European Instrument Pilot

First published in 2008 by
PPL/IR Europe,
The Business Centre
Llangarron
Ross-on-Wye
Herefordshire
HR9 6PG
United Kingdom

ISBN 978-0-9559043-0-1

Typeset in Adobe Garamond Pro 11/13.2 pt

Printed and bound in Great Britain by
Biddles Ltd, Kings Lynn

European
Instrument Pilot

PPL/IR EUROPE

Acknowledgements

This book would not have been possible without the assistance of a wide number of people, including:

Articles for publication:
- Vasa Babic
- Anthony Bowles
- Steven Copeland
- Paul Draper
- Christof Edel
- Nigel Everett
- Peter Holy
- Robert Lough
- Anthony Mollison
- Linda Mollison
- Timothy Nathan
- Judith Niechcial
- Stephen Niechcial
- Jeff Pearce
- David Sowray
- Jim Thorpe

The photographs on pages 55 to 62 and 151 to 158 illustrate a small selection of the wide variety of aircraft types and destinations flown to by members of *PPL/IR Europe* and have kindly been supplied by the above members with additional photos by:
- Cameron Aitken
- Peter Bondar
- David Findon
- Ole Henriksen
- Judith Niechcial
- Andy Reohorn
- Alan South
- Sally Turner
- Phil Wadsworth
- Philip Whiteman

Cover photograph Cessna 421C supplied by Vasa Babic.

Typesetting by Paul Turner and illustrations by Sally Jane Turner, www.sally-jane.com.

Contents

Foreword

The intelligent observer discovering flying for the first time might reasonably expect it to be a scientific activity with well understood best practice founded in long years of practical experience. To a large extent this is true but there remain a surprising number of enduring half truths and downright myths. Instrument flight, and in particular the process of obtaining the instrument rating has attracted its fair share of misleading folk wisdom. Perhaps this is because, unlike wars, where the victors write the history the most interesting pilot stories are told by those who found the learning process problematic.

It is true that the single pilot instrument rating will be the most challenging test a private pilot and probably even a commercial pilot will ever experience. It is not as though any of the individual skills are impossibly hard. You may have good basic flying skills, you can use radio aids to establish your position, and you can read an approach plate or deal with ATC communications. The hard part is delivering all these things simultaneously while flying to tight accuracy standards. However that's not the whole problem. You sometimes need to do this in spite of distractions such as adverse weather, technical problems or unhelpful ATC clearances. In the test situation the examiner cannot safely reproduce these potentially dangerous distractions but the test is designed to allow you to demonstrate your ability while under pressure in different ways. A much criticised requirement of the UK instrument rating initial flight test is to fly precise holding patterns. This skill will be largely irrelevant to your future flying in the real world and so can seem arcane and unnecessary. However if you can develop the competence and sense of priorities to enable you to handle this complex task the abilities will stand you in good stead when you need to fly accurately while in turbulence with the distraction of a nervous passenger or some aircraft fault. Your IR gives you the privilege of operating in an environment where most of the other participants are flying more capable aircraft with the benefit of having two crew. A PPL/IR needs to go beyond flying safely. He or she also needs to be able to operate well within their capabilities so that as far as humanly possible they fit seamlessly into the IFR system and do not represent a hindrance to other airspace users. Most PPL holders will have the academic skills and basic flying ability which would enable them to reach IR test standards. Possibly a lesser proportion will have the motivation, attitude time and money which will enable them firstly to reach and then maintain an acceptable skill and currency level.

The decision as to whether all this effort is worthwhile must in the end be quite personal. The rationale for getting the rating is most often expressed in terms of the increased utility it provides, perhaps for some business travel purpose. Of course this utility increase is true but I suspect a far more common and perhaps more important motive is not so often talked about. This is about the challenge and the sense of achievement and personal satisfaction to be gained from acquiring the necessary competence. Certainly the flight home from my initial instrument rating test was one of the high spots of my whole life, far surpassing the euphoria of the first solo. I know that I am far from alone in feeling this way. Since that time the IR has given me the chance to do some of the functional flying we expect from it but more importantly it has enabled me to make some long and interesting trips, make many new friends and experience some really magic moments.

As you try for the tenth time to roll out within five degrees on the inbound track to the beacon under the despairing eye of your instructor you will question your sanity. The day you transit serenely overhead Heathrow in a vivid blue sky bound for some pleasant destination watching commercial traffic climbing and descending through a solid cloud deck below you will know the effort and even the pain was very worthwhile indeed.

Jim Thorpe,
Chairman *PPL/IR Europe*

Introduction

I qualified for my basic PPL in August 1971 in the ubiquitous Cessna 150. In the following months, I got checked out on a 172 and Cherokee 180 and did some instrument work and radio navigation cross country work with my PPL instructor which I see from my log book included my first landing at Gatwick. In June 1972, I set off for a tour round France in a rented 172 with two friends. We had various adventures, gastronomic and otherwise and it was only later that I learnt that one of my friends had resisted a large inducement from his parents not to come with me. Two recollections stand out from an aviation viewpoint; first a tedious two day delay leaving Perpignan because of a thin stratus overcast at around 400 feet and the refusal of the aerodrome controller to permit a VFR departure northwards up the coast to where better weather existed. The second recollection was climbing out of Bordeaux for Chartres in hazy anticyclonic conditions and deciding to turn back because I could not see where I was going. The met man at Bordeaux was bemused at my return because all his reports spoke of CAVOK. We tried again an hour or so later and by then the warming day had lifted the inversion so horizontal visibility through the haze had improved sufficiently to make the flight quite straightforward. I had yet to learn that climbing through the inversion layer solved all visibility problems.

Back in England, I resolved to get the then relatively new IMC rating and did this in the autumn of 1972. In those days, simple training aircraft did not have ILS or even the now, much maligned, ADF; VDF letdowns were the order of the day (and quite a laugh too) interspersed with the occasional PAR approach to Farnborough when the RAF controllers were not too busy.

In 1973 I acquired my first aeroplane, a simple Cessna and this together with the IMCR kept me happy for a while. Looking back at my log book, I see a number of instrument hours recorded over the following couple of years, some of which related to flights outside the UK. I became conscious that while the IMCR was a valuable extension to my flying in the UK, it had its limitations not least of which it did not work outside the UK so that occasionally I was grounded at a continental airport in conditions that would have been quite manageable in the UK. Thus with family encouragement, I embarked on training for the full IR. This meant doing the distance learning course with Oxford Air Training School over the winter of 1974/75 working in the evenings and at weekends before starting the flying training in April and passing the flying test in May. Those days were heady times leaving London at 7 am driving to Oxford, doing one or two training flights before returning to London to do some work. Luckily I worked for an understanding firm who allowed me to work flexitime, otherwise then unheard of.

Having achieved an IR rating on my licence, life was then rather an anti-climax. True, I could now get in and out of continental airports in relatively benign IFR conditions and this was certainly useful on occasions. However my aircraft was unsuitable for serious touring and the need to further my professional career, together with getting married and starting a family meant that aviation had to take a back seat for a while. We usually managed a short continental tour each year and I kept the IR rating going on annual renewal but there were certainly times when I wondered whether all the effort and expense had been worthwhile in terms of the real practical use I made of the rating.

Family and business prospered and by 1987 I was able to buy my second aircraft, a Grumman Tiger which I kept until a few months ago before changing to a Cirrus SR22. My Tiger was a big step up; it came airways equipped and apart from replacing the unreliable autopilot with an early S-TEC unit and putting in a stormscope, little work was required on the aircraft over the years other than routine maintenance. It cruised at around 130 Kts TAS at 8,000 feet with a still air IFR range of around 450 NM. I could now do sensible journeys to Europe with frequent business trips from my then base of Elstree to Germany, Luxembourg and northern France. A couple of years later, we bought a house in SW Scotland and thus began a regular commute from Elstree to Carlisle which continues to this day. European business flying waned as the nineties progressed and again had it not been for my Scottish commute, I may have questioned the need to keep an aircraft. However the state of the West Coast main line and the M6 (both then and now) ensured that my aviation thrived. Late in the nineties, we moved up to Scotland and the direction of the commute reversed.

There were a number of reasons for selling my Tiger and buying a Cirrus which I expand on in a later article "Transitioning to a glass cockpit". In summary the extra speed shaves off useful time on my London run, more useful in some respects is the

Cirrus' easy ability to cruise in the low teen flight levels which can often provide a comfortable VMC ride on top of lower convective cloud, something not possible in the Tiger where any level above FL90 was a bit of a struggle and the additional range is also a considerable advantage for longer distance touring.

So why, you may ask have I given a potted history of my flying résumé? There is nothing very special in it; many others have done far longer and more exotic journeys. The reason is simply that there are probably many who have followed a similar path – achieving a PPL, then wondering how to use it and progress from there; getting an IMCR or Night Rating both of which open up new vistas but also disclose new limitations, whether on personal skills or the flying characteristics of one's aircraft. Setting one's goal for an IR, perhaps the pinnacle of achievement in terms of flying with the commercial boys in controlled airspace, only then to find problems in using or keeping the rating up for the mundane reasons that affect us all, or certainly most of us, is more common than some may imagine.

The objects of this publication are several and it is divided into a number of sections. **Section 1** has a number of articles on flying training in what is by no means a simple legal environment, presently made more complex by the forthcoming transition to the EASA flight licensing regime. Linda and Anthony Mollison set out the current requirements for obtaining and revalidating a JAA IR while Christof Edel explains how it is still practical with hard work and good organisation to obtain the JAA IR without having to take a sabbatical away from job and family. Peter Holy explains what has become a popular alternative of obtaining the FAA IR operating on an N registered aircraft while Vasa Babic provides guidance on more advanced training and qualifications.

Section 2 deals with the selection of suitable aircraft for IFR operations. Timothy Nathan, one of our most experienced members, sets out a list of basic choices an aspiring operator should consider and discusses the pros and cons of each. Nigel Everett then provides another view on selection criteria particularly in terms of upgrading systems in older aircraft while Steven and I provide a more in depth view of subjects aired by Timothy, namely the use of oxygen in General Aviation and transitioning to a glass cockpit respectively.

Section 3 deals with a variety of operational topics. The first article which appeared recently in Instrument Pilot is Vasa Babic's seminal work on Self-flown GA IFR transport in Europe: a User's Guide. While at first sight, one may think that much of what Vasa writes relates only to the expensive high performance end of the market, a careful read will show that most of Vasa's topics are relevant to any IFR GA flight in Europe to some degree. Specific aspects are then developed in further articles; David Sowray provides guidance on flight planning away from base, Jim Thorpe on the preparation and maintenance of your aircraft for IFR flight and Robert Lough shares some advice on icing scenarios.

Section 4 brings elements of the first three sections together by three *PPL/IR Europe* members describing particular European journeys they have made in their own aircraft. First Jeff Pearce writes on the *PPL/IR Europe* 2006 fly out to Tunisia and Sicily in what has now become an annual event, designed to bring ten aircraft or so and their crews together to undertake a trip that individually they may feel less comfortable in making. The 2007 trip was to Spain and Morocco while the 2008 trip is scheduled to visit Scandinavia and the Baltic. Next, two members describe solo trips; first Peter Holy takes us to Prague in his TB20 and then Stephen Niechcial takes us to the Greek Islands in his Tiger routing through some wild country on his way.

The epilogue has an article by Paul Draper, a former chairman of *PPL/IR Europe*, setting out what the organisation does and seeks to achieve and concludes with Jim Thorpe crystal ball gazing on the future of the IR.

What we seek to achieve by this publication is to encourage pilots whether or not they be *PPL/IR Europe* members to gain additional qualifications, experience and enjoyment and thereby become safer pilots. We also hope that non *PPL/IR Europe* members may be encouraged to become members of an organisation which has already succeeded in establishing valuable links with EASA officials in the run in to the EASA licence transition period which is going to affect all of us to some degree.

Each article is separately authored and some authors have contributed more than one article. We have not sought to mould authors' individual literary styles into one cohesive house style because one of the objects of this work is to offer to the reader a wide range of experience from people with very diverse aviation backgrounds.

Lastly I must highlight one important warning which is placed in each issue of Instrument Pilot where some of the articles you read may have first appeared. The authors are essentially amateur pilots and while reasonable efforts have been taken to check the accuracy of factual statements made by individual authors, no reliance should be placed upon such statements unless they are independently checked and verified by the appropriate authority. Neither the officers of *PPL/IR Europe* nor the authors accept any responsibility for any misstatement or opinion set out in this work.

And as a postscript, was all the work I did in obtaining the rating in 1974/75 worthwhile? Certainly I think so, not only from the intellectual satisfaction of the exercise but from the many practical occasions that it enabled me to maintain a reliable travel schedule even with a comparatively simple SEP aircraft.

Anthony Bowles,
January 2008

Glossary of aviation terms

AAL	above aerodrome level
ACAS	aircraft collision avoidance system
AD	airworthiness directive
ADF	automatic direction finder
ADS-B	automatic dependent surveillance-broadcast
AIM	aeronautical information manual
AMSL	above mean sea level
ANO	UK Air Navigation Order 2005
AoA	angle of attack
AOC	air operator's certificate
AOPA	Aircraft Owners & Pilots Association
ASA	Aviation Supplies & Academics, Inc.
ATC	air traffic control
ATP	airline transport pilot (also, ATPL airline transport pilot licence)
ATS	air traffic services
ATZ	aerodrome traffic zone
BFR	FAA biennial flight review
BRNAV	basic area navigation
C	centigrade
CAA	Civil Aviation Authority
CAT	commercial air transport
CAT I, II or III	category of instrument landing system
CAVOK	ceiling and visibility OK (or CAVU, ceiling and visibility unlimited)
CRI	class rating instructor
CPL/IR	commercial pilot's licence/instrument rating
CDI	course deviation indicator
CFI	certified flight instructor (or chief flying instructor)
CFII	certified instrument flight instructor
CFMU	central flow management unit
CRI	class rating instructor
CRM	crew resource management (previously cockpit resource management)
CTA	control area
CTOT	calculated takeoff time
CTZ	control zone
DCT	direct
DME	distance measuring equipment
EGT	exhaust gas temperature
EASA	European Aviation Safety Agency
EFATO	engine failure after take-off

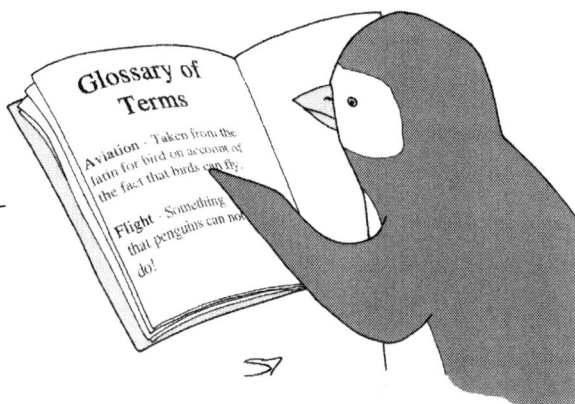

EFIS	electronic flight information system
EGPWS	enhanced ground-proximity warning system
EOBT	estimated off-block time
ETA	estimated time of arrival
EU	European Union
FAA	Federal Aviation Authority
FADEC	full authority digital engine control
FAR	federal aviation regulation
FCL	flight crew licensing
FD	flight director
FI	flight instructor
FL	flight level
FMS	flight management system (or flight manual supplement)
FNPT	flight and navigation procedures trainer
FPL	flight plan
GA	general aviation
GAR	general aviation report
GFS	global forecast system
GPS	global positioning system
HSI	horizontal situation indicator
IAP	instrument approach procedure
ICAO	International Civil Aviation Organisation
IFPS	integrated initial flight plan processing system
IFR	instrument flight rules
IAS	indicated airspeed
ILS	instrument landing system
IMC	instrument meteorological conditions
IPC	instrument proficiency check
IR	instrument rating
IRE	instrument rating examiner
IRI	instrument rating instructor
IRR	instrument rating renewal
JAA	Joint Aviation Authority
JAR	joint aviation requirements
Kts	knots (i.e. 1 nautical mile per hour)
LASORS	licensing, administration and standardisation; operating requirements and safety. A publication of the UK CAA
MEA	minimum enroute altitude
MEI	multi-engine instructor
MET	meteorology (also multi engine turbine)
METAR	meteorological terminal air report
MFD	multi-function display
MEP	multi-engine piston
MHz	megahertz

MSA	minimum sector altitude
NATS	National Air Traffic Services Ltd
NDB	non-directional beacon
NOTAM	notices to airmen
OCA	obstacle clearance altitude
PFD	primary flight display
POH	pilot's operating handbook
PPL/IR	private pilot's licence/instrument rating
PRNAV	precision area navigation
QNH	barometric pressure at sea level, corrected for airport elevation
RAIM	receiver autonomous integrity monitoring
RBI	relative bearing indicator
RMI	radio magnetic indicator
RNAV	area navigation
ROC	rate of climb
ROD	rate of descent
SET	single engine turbine
SID	standard instrument departure route
SEP	single-engine piston
SESAR	single European sky air traffic research project
SEVIS	student and exchange visitor information system (US Immigration and Naturalization Service)
SOP	standard operating procedures
STAR	standard terminal arrival route
STC	supplemental type certificate
TAA	technically advanced aircraft
TAF	terminal area forecast
TAS	traffic advisory system (also true airspeed)
TAWS	terrain awareness and warning system
TCAS	traffic alert and collision avoidance system
TIT	turbine inlet temperature
TKS	type of de-icing system (taken from the initial letters of the three companies that collaborated in the design of the system: Tecalemit, Kilfrost, and Sheepbridge Stokes)
TSA	Transportation Security Administration
VDF	very high frequency direction finding system
VLA	very light aircraft
VLJ	very light jet
VOR	very high frequency omni-directional range
VMC	visual meteorological conditions
VSO	aircraft stalling speed in the landing configuration
WX	weather

SECTION 1

Pilot training

Section Contents

1   Getting the JAA PPL/IR (A)

By Linda Mollison

Things to be aware of

Difference between countries

Although the introduction of the Joint Aviation Authority Regulations in 2000 was an attempt to harmonise all aviation related rules in most of Europe, regional differences still exist, particularly in the area of conversion of non-JAA licences/ratings.

This is partly due to the fact that although JAA rules may have been implemented by the JAA they have not necessarily become law in individual countries (i.e. they have not been implemented into a country's Air Navigation Order), and partly due to the fact that individual countries have interpreted the rules in different ways.

> **JAR FCL 1.016**
> *An applicant for a JAR-FCL licence and IR, if applicable, already holding at least an equivalent licence issued in accordance with ICAO Annex 1 by a non-JAA state shall meet all the requirements of JAR-FCL, except that the requirements of course duration, number of lessons and specific training hours may be reduced.*
>
> *The Authority may be guided as to the credits to be granted on the basis of a recommendation from an appropriate training organisation.*

For example, when it comes to converting a non-JAA IR to a JAA one, the JAA training requirements are quite vague (see side-bar on previous page).

This has been interpreted in different ways by different countries, e.g. in the UK, minimum course hours have been laid down by the UK CAA. It is my understanding that in Belgium, training is on an as required basis, i.e. no minimum hours, and in Germany the training requirements are laid down by individual flight training organisations. Other countries may even have different rules.

Where regional differences are known they will be covered, but if you are planning on doing the ground or the flying training in a country other than the UK, please check with your national authority that their rules are the same as the UK ones.

Changes afoot

This chapter covers the **existing** arrangements for getting a JAR PPL(A). A JAA study has been recently carried out which looked at both the potential future theoretical study/examination requirements. This study recommended that the theoretical examinations should become much simpler in terms of content. This has been incorporated into JAA, but has not yet been implemented into the law in every country. It has not yet been implemented in the UK.

The flying side has also been looked at. JAA has changed to allow training to be split into a ten hour Basic Instrument Flight Module (BIFM) and a 40 (single-engine) or 45 hour (multi-engine) Procedural Instrument Flight Module (PIFM). This may have been implemented in other European countries, but it has still not been incorporated into the UK ANO. As yet we do not have a timescale on when the UK ANO will be changed.

European Aviation Safety Association (EASA)

The governing body for European pilots' licences/ratings will shortly change from JAA to EASA. Under EASA, all existing and new rules will become law immediately in all European countries signed up to EASA, i.e. regional differences will be no longer be allowed. Version 7 of JAA is being taken as the base document for EASA. The UK is currently on version 5, with some elements of version 7, but will upgrade fully to version 7 before the EASA implementation date (currently mid-April 2008). This chapter is based on the current UK CAA implementation of JAR FCL.

Medical requirements

You need to have a JAA Class One medical, or a Class Two medical PLUS an audiogram, in order to get your IR issued. For obvious reasons, it is not recommended that you start your training until after you have obtained your medical.

Theoretical studies/examinations

You are allowed to do the theoretical knowledge training in one JAA country and the flying training in another, providing the two countries have a reciprocal arrangement. If you wish to do this, you will need to get written permission from each country (in advance) and you will have to provide the country which is issuing the rating with copies of both these letters, plus a copy of the approval certificate from the theoretical knowledge provider.

In addition, neither the ground school, nor the flying training has to be done in the country which issued the JAA PPL.

I advise anyone who is considering training in different JAA countries to confirm this is acceptable to all the countries involved before you start any training.

The seven theoretical knowledge exams consist of the following:

- Aircraft General;
- IFR Communications;
- Air Law & ATC Procedures;
- Meteorology;
- Flight Performance and Planning;
- Navigation.
- Human Performance and Limitations;

In the UK, you have to undertake a formal course before you take the exams, but this can be done by distance learning.

Officially, you have to do around 300 hours of study. This consists of two or three modules, each followed by a number of days of full time revision held at the premises of the theoretical knowledge provider, usually during the week before the exams. The exams can only be taken at the CAA premises at Gatwick.

You have to have passed all of your exams within 18 months of the date of your first exam pass.

If you already hold a current and valid ICAO IR (i.e. an IR issued by a non-JAA country that has not passed its expiry date) training is on an as required basis, and the requirement to attend the revision courses is determined by the theoretical knowledge provider.

There are currently only three ground schools in the UK who run the JAA PPL/IR (A) theoretical knowledge courses. These are:

- Ground Training Services (Bournemouth)
  Tel: + 44 (0) 1202 580809
  email: roger@gtserv.co.uk

- Aviation Training Services (Cranfield)
  Tel: + 44 (0) 1234 757969
  email: information@cranfieldaviation.co.uk

- Atlantic Flight Training (Coventry)
  Tel: + 44 (0) 845 4500530
  email: enquiries@flyaft.com

Pilots not based in the UK will need to contact their JAA authority for a list of ground schools that provide this training in their country.

Flight training

Pre-course/licence issue requirements

You need to have passed all of your ground exams before you take your IR skill test. This is not a requirement for starting the course, but we strongly recommend that you do not start the course until you have passed all the exams.

This is due to the fact that the examinations are only held every other month so, if you fail one or more exams it will be two months before you get the results of your next set of exams. If you are doing the flying training full-time, you will have finished your course well before this, so you will have a gap between finishing your course and taking your flight test. This will probably mean that you will need some revision flight training which will obviously cost you extra.

You also need the following to start your course:

↷ to be the holder of an ICAO PPL(A), including a night qualification, or

↷ to be the holder of an ICAO CPL(A).

You also need to be the holder of a UK JAA Flight Radio Telephony Operator's Licence. In the UK, this has to have been issued by the UK CAA.

In order to get your IR issued you need to have at least 50 hours cross country flight time as PIC in aeroplanes or helicopters, of which at least 10 hours shall be in aeroplanes.

In addition, if a multi-engine IR is required you need to have undertaken a multi-engine piston class rating (MEP) course prior to commencing the IR course although you do not need to have passed the test. If you are undertaking your MEP course immediately before you start your IR course it is often advantageous to wait until you are most of the way though your IR course before you take your MEP Skills Test.

You should note that, although the requirement to commence the course is an ICAO licence rather than a JAA licence, you will be required to convert this to a JAA licence in order to be able to get your rating issued.

Flying training

The training course must be done at a flight training organisation which is JAA approved to run IR courses.

Training requirements differ depending upon whether you already hold a current and valid ICAO IR (i.e. an IR issued by a non-JAA country that has not passed its expiry date) or not.

If your ICAO IR has expired it may well be worth your while renewing it so that you can convert it. The full multi IR flying course is 55 hours (single-engine 50 hours); the UK conversion course is 15 hours!

No credit is given for a UK IMC rating.

Non ICAO IR holders

You need to decide initially whether you want to do a single or a multi-engine IR.

Single-engine IR

⌒ This is a minimum 50 hour course (45 hours if you hold an ICAO CPL(A)).

⌒ Up to 20 hours of the 50 hour course can be completed in a suitably approved FNPT1 simulator.

⌒ Up to 35 hours of the 50 hour course can be completed in a suitably approved simulator (up to 30 hours of the 45 hour course).

⌒ A minimum of 15 hours must be completed in the single-engined aircraft.

Multi-engine IR

⌒ This is a minimum 55 hour course (50 hours if you hold an ICAO CPL(A)).

⌒ Up to 25 hours of the 55 hour course can be completed in a suitably approved FNPT1 simulator.

⌒ Up to 40 hours of the 55 hour course can be completed in a suitably approved FNPT2 simulator (up to 35 hours of the 50 hour course).

⌒ A minimum of 15 hours must be completed in the multi- engined aircraft.

Single-engine to multi-engine upgrade

⌒ You can upgrade a single-engine IR to a multi-engine one (you need to do a multi-engine piston class rating first).

⌒ This is a minimum five hour course of which three hours can be completed in a suitably approved FNPT2 simulator.

Holder of an ICAO IR

A holder of an ICAO IR is allowed to do an abridged flying training course. The number of training hours will depend upon whether you want to convert:

⌒ a single-engine ICAO IR to a single-engine JAA IR;

⌒ a single-engine ICAO IR to a multi-engine JAA IR;

⌒ a multi-engine ICAO IR to a multi-engine JAA IR.

It will also depend upon in which JAA country you are doing your IR, and which country is going to be issuing your IR (normally the country which originally issued your PPL).

As stated above, different countries have interpreted the JAA rules in different ways. It is even more complicated in that if you are trying to add, say, a Belgian IR to a UK PPL, I understand that the UK CAA requires you to do the minimum hours course as defined in their rules. They will not accept training on an as required basis which is the Belgian interpretation of JAA.

Rather than stating what the conversion requirements are in each of the 40 or so countries who are members of JAA, I will state the UK requirements only. Non-UK members are advised to check with their own Civil Aviation Authority for their conversion requirements.

Single-engine ICAO IR to a single-engine JAA IR

⌒ This is a minimum 15 hour course.

⌒ Up to five hours of the 15 hour course can be completed in a suitably approved FNPT1 simulator.

⌒ Up to ten hours of the 15 hour course can be completed in a suitably approved FNPT2 simulator.

⌒ A minimum of five hours must be completed in the multi-engined aircraft (ten if an FNPT1 simulator is used).

Single-engine ICAO IR to a multi-engine JAA IR

There are three options on how you can do this.

Option 1:

⌒ This is a minimum 15 hour single-engine course of which:

⌒ Up to five hours can be completed in a suitably approved FNPT1 simulator.

⌒ Up to ten hours can be completed in a suitably approved FNPT2 simulator.

⌒ A minimum of five hours must be completed in the multi-engined aircraft (ten if an FNPT1 simulator is used).

⌒ Followed by a minimum five hour multi-engine course of which up to three hours can be completed in a suitably approved FNPT2 simulator.

Option 2:

⌒ This is a minimum 20 hour multi-engine course of which:

⌒ Up to 13 hours can be completed in a suitably approved FNPT2 simulator.

⌒ A minimum of seven hours must be completed in the multi-engined aircraft.

Option 3:

⌒ This is a minimum 15 hour course which must all be completed in a multi-engined aircraft, i.e. no FNPT1 or FNPT2 time allowed.

For all options, you must either hold an ICAO multi rating, or have completed the MEP class rating course before commencing your IR conversion training.

Other conversions
There are also rules for other conversions, e.g. ICAO IR(H) to JAR IR(A), JAR IR(H) to JAR IR(A) etc. The UK rules can be found on the UK CAA website (www.srg.caa. co.uk) under Personnel Licensing, Flight Crew Licensing, LASORS, section E. Rules in other JAA countries should be available on their CAA's website.

The skill test
The skill test is carried out as follows:
   You will be required to depart from the airfield where you are taking the test and join the airways to fly to another airport. You will do either an NDB (or a VOR), or an ILS approach at this other airfield. The ILS may be procedural or vectored. You will then go off and do some general handling/emergency procedures, after which you will return to the original airfield to do the other type of approach, followed by a visual circuit to land. If you are doing a multi-engined IR one of the approaches will be asymmetric.
   For the single-engine to multi-engine upgrade you are required to do another IR skill test with a CAA full time examiner, but the test only consists of approaches (asymmetric), i.e. no airways work.
   The skill test can only be done in a JAA country and (in the UK) can only be done by a full-time CAA examiner. It is understood that some other JAA countries, e.g. Spain, allow authorised examiners to undertake initial IR tests.

Using your own aircraft
It is possible to do the training/test in your own aircraft. It will need to be approved by the JAA for the test, but this is not too complicated. Basically, you will need instrument screens (temporary cardboard ones are acceptable), an approved checklist and a minimum equipment fit, e.g. two altimeters. Your school should be able to help you with all of this. And of course you will need to pay the Authority for this (around £150 in the UK).

The other thing to check before you decide to use your own aircraft is the cost of landing fees at the airport where you are planning to do your training. At around 2.5 landings/approaches per hour of flying training this can soon add up.

Part-time vs. full-time

The flying course will take anything from 5-6 weeks upwards. Ideally this should be completed on a full-time basis. I appreciate that businessmen find it very difficult to take that length of time off work.

If you cannot manage to train on a full-time basis, please bear in mind the following:

- You need to have applied to get your rating issued within 36 months of your last exam pass date otherwise you will have to do all the exams again.

- Trying to fit training sessions in after a full working day does not work because:

  a) you are tired and

  b) you are probably still thinking about work.

- Trying to fit training sessions in when you get a moment spare, without pre-booking, does not work because:

  a) you are likely to get whichever instructor happens to be around, which will mean potentially a different instructor for each flight and

  b) you are unlikely to get enough 'spare' moments.

The longer elapsed time you take, the more training you will require, and the more it will cost you.

If you have to do the training on a part-time basis, sit down with the school and work out a programme. Try and insist on the same instructor for each flight, or maybe a primary instructor plus one back-up.

Choosing a school

Each JAA country will have its own list of approved IR flight training organisations. There are currently 28 approved IR schools in the UK. Some are one man bands, some are (relatively) large. The CAA IR school list (www.caa.co.uk, standards document 31) does NOT say it all! Make the right decision first time - changing schools is NOT easy! Personal recommendation is a very good starting point.

Make a short-list and visit the schools shortlisted

- By appointment;

- Talk to instructors;

⌒ Talk to current students.

⌒ Ask for reference names (other PPL/IRers)

Checklist

Use the following personal checklist before committing to a start date for flight training.

1. Have you passed all the ground exams? (see pre-course/licence issue requirements above).

2. Have you the money available? Not just the course price, also:

    ⌒ aircraft hire for test;

    ⌒ CAA test fee (over £700 in the UK!);

    ⌒ landings and approaches (both home and away);

    ⌒ fuel surcharges;

    ⌒ etc, etc etc.

    Such extras could add as much as **10%** to the course price plus you will need a contingency of say **20%**.

3. Have you the time available? You will need a minimum of 6-8 weeks allowing for bad weather and overruns, more if part-time.

4. Is seasonal weather significant?

    ⌒ Icing (does the school have de-iced aircraft);

    ⌒ Poor visibility and low cloud (minima for single-engine aircraft is higher than for multis).

5. Does the location have:

    ⌒ Resident CAA examiners (otherwise you need to relocate to another airfield for the test – additional cost plus less familiarity with airfield)?

    ⌒ Navigation aids (ILS/NDB) (otherwise you need to relocate for training)?

6. Is it wise to split the training e.g. USA/UK?

There are several JAA approved (mainly UK CAA approved) flight training organisations in the States who offer 'cheap' IR options, commencing your training in the US, and completing it (normally 15 hours training) in the UK (you have to do your IR test in a JAA country). Beware this option. The airspace and R/T is very different in the US and they do not have NDBs. In our experience the 15 hours is not adequate and most people taking this option end up spending at least as much as they would have done (plus aggro!) if they had completed all of their training in Europe.

7. Is the school financially viable?

This issue needs to be taken very seriously. A large number of flight training organisations have gone bust over the years, and many students have lost large sums of money.

A training organisation seeking approval is required by the JAA to satisfy them that sufficient funding is available to conduct courses of flying or ground training to the approved standards, but prospective trainees should be aware that this does not imply any protection of fees paid to training organisations.

Methods of paying for courses of training can vary. For example, some organisations may require a lump sum payment in advance, some may offer a discount for payment in advance, others may accept staged payments. Whatever method is used, you are strongly advised to give careful consideration to any financial agreement before becoming committed. 'Pay as you go' or via an escrow account.

8   What is the school's first time pass rate?

First time, not first series. Some schools quote first series pass rate which means two attempts at the test, not one. Read the small print. It is wise also to check with some current students of the school what they think the school's pass rate is. Pass rates are not published other than a national pass rate (currently around 50% first time). Schools quoting 95% pass rates may be referring to the first series!

9. Will I get continuity of instructor? i.e. one instructor for the course.

10. How many IR instructors?

⌒   Full-time/part-time. If they only have one, what happens if he becomes ill? If they only have part-time instructors, it may be difficult to keep to the same instructor.

⌒   Hours builders/career instructors. Hours builders tend to be young and inexperienced and many are not really interested in instructing. They are simply waiting for that airline job to come along.

11. How many simulators and IFR aircraft does the school have of the type you want to use? If they only have one, what happens if it breaks down? Do they have a standard lay-out? Different cockpit layouts in different aircraft, and between the simulator and the aircraft is very confusing.

12. Is the school approved to carry out IR instruction both in the FNPT1/FNPT2 simulators and in the aircraft (separate approvals)? Ask to see the approval certificate(s).

The IR is a demanding course – even for those with above-average skill and learning ability. Your full attention is definitely required!

Helpful publications

The following publications may be of some use:

JAR-FCL 1 (not available on-line, can be purchased, should be available at any FTO). General details regarding this publication are given on the JAA website www.jaa.nl.

LASORS (UK only). A document produced every year by the UK CAA. Available online at www.caa.co.uk, under Flight Crew Licensing.

The author is a Director at Professional Air Training Ltd, Bournemouth. The Company specialises in instrument rating training and renewals, especially for the PPL/IR.

2 JAA IR revalidation

By Anthony Mollison

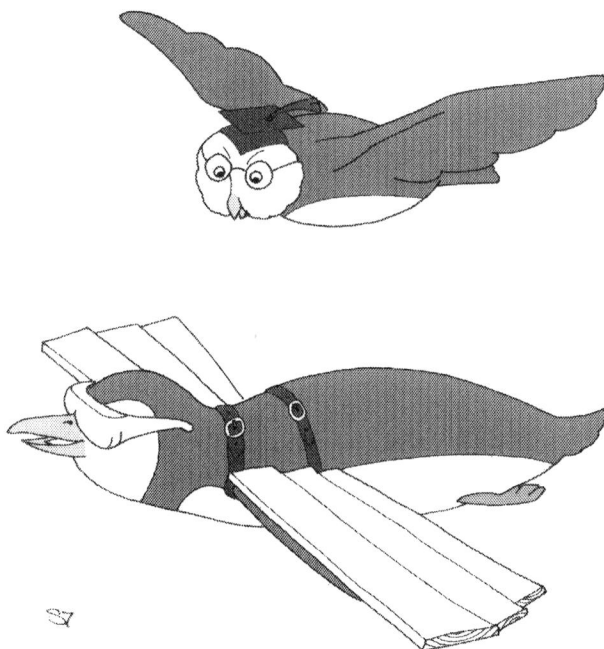

IRR examiner Anthony Mollison tells us how the JAA instrument rating check ride looks from the right hand seat

First, most examiners are human! What does this mean? It means for a start that they have to keep current and to go through the same revalidation process as everybody else. They too make the odd error and sometimes perform less than perfectly (I don't believe it, I hear you say!), so they should have a reasonably humble and helpful approach to the examining role. Bear in mind also that under the now current rules the examiner must hold valid and appropriate instructor and licence/rating qualifications, e.g. a training captain on 747s may not examine you unless he also holds the qualifications appropriate to your type of aircraft (or you fly 747s).

Another thing to bear in mind is that although the instrument rating check is a longer flight than it used to be and now includes, quite rightly, limited panel and a non-precision approach; it is in other respects easier to pass. Not that I am saying that examiners have become softer these days, but there seems to be a more flexible attitude. For instance, the CAA flight examiners handbook states under a revalidation that the examiner, at his discretion, may repeat items in flight.

However, this is realistically limited to one or two repeats, so don't expect that he or she will allow you to go round and round gradually running out of fuel, whilst you desperately try to fly an ILS to within limits.

Proficiency check rather than test

The examiner must of course bend over backwards to be fair and must take a positive view. The IR proficiency check is increasingly becoming a 'value added training exercise', rather than just a tick (or a cross) in the boxes.

Political correctness has moved into the flying world, as elsewhere. The trend is towards limiting the use of the 'f' word, and moving towards such expressions as 'not yet satisfactory, so that I am unable to sign your licence today'.

So how do you give yourself the best chance of passing your IR proficiency check? I probably should not say this, but your check flight is going to be easier if you fly a known route and approaches, and with a known examiner. However, I would suggest that this is rather a negative way of thinking and it is better to change examiners and routes from time to time. Alternate revalidations in an FNPT II can provide an excellent opportunity to tackle a new route and approaches (maybe reflecting an IFR flight that you intend to undertake before too long). Be as prepared as you can for the day. Book a date which will allow you enough time for preparation, and have a reserve date (presumably within your rating validity period) as a precaution.

It should be possible to agree with the examiner in advance a route and approaches and other details. You should be able to fill in an outline plog in advance, plan the likely approaches and alternatives, and think through the whole exercise in detail. Fill in the flight plan and agree who is going to file it. Make sure that your paperwork, including medical, is up to date and to hand.

And practice! This could be on your pc (personal computer rather than political correctness), in a simulator or in an aircraft. IFR flying is very demanding and though you may have regular opportunities to fly routes and approaches, there will be other items, for example engine failure after take-off or limited panel, for which you are likely to need a bit of refresher training from a good instructor.

On the day, arrive early and relaxed. Don't schedule a business meeting beforehand, so that you arrive late, tired and fraught! Also, avoid flying late in the day, particularly at night, when such items as reading the plates and writing down clearances become more difficult.

The briefing

The examiner's briefing will include the following:

- Check of your licence (and you have the right to check the examiner's – no point in being examined by someone whose examiner rating has lapsed);

- Is the weather acceptable? (Your choice provided the flight can be flown within legal limits);

⌒ Examiner and examinee's responsibilities i.e. most of the workload for the former and observation for the latter;

⌒ Who does R/T and when;

⌒ Exercises to be done (in chronological order);

⌒ Checks and drills required;

⌒ Planned speeds;

⌒ Who does what in an actual emergency?;

⌒ Everything understood and agreed?

The flight

For the flight itself, you could take a packet of mints to break the ice. Concentrate primarily on aviating = flying the aircraft. Correct altimetry and accurate altitude or level maintenance (+/- 100 ft) is a very sound basis for any flight. I fly with so many people who are desperate to get in a non-urgent radio call, whilst going into a spiral dive or heading towards a wheels up landing. Try to forget about the examiner.

Don't be too self-conscious. Assume that you are doing fine and, if something goes wrong, forget it and get on with the next task - and do that better!

After the flight, the overall assessment of your performance should be forthcoming almost immediately, followed by detailed feedback. Try to learn from the examiner's experience (and he also should be willing to learn). It is diplomatic, if nothing else, to make it clear that you are taking any constructive comments on board. The whole point of the exercise is to increase the safety of your IFR flying.

Good luck with your next revalidation or renewal. I hope that it will be to standard and a useful learning exercise.

Some useful facts

⌒ The IR is revalidated when it has not reached its expiry date. If it has expired it is renewed.

⌒ The instrument rating attached to a CAA or JAA licence needs to be revalidated by a proficiency check every 12 months to the day in order to continue to use its privileges.

⌒ Proficiency check is the modern version of an instrument rating renewal test, carried out by a so called class rating examiner with IR renewal privileges. Note: strictly speaking the term revalidation is used when the proficiency check is completed within the validity period, otherwise it is a renewal.

⌒ This proficiency check may be brought forward by up to three months without any loss of the validity period - same principle as the 28 days for your car's M.O.T.

⌒ If the IR is not revalidated before its expiry date, you must do the proficiency check in an aircraft; if you revalidate it before its expiry date each alternate revalidation may be done in an FNPT2 simulator.

⌒ If the IR is not revalidated on time, the privileges attached to the rating may not be exercised until such time as the proficiency check is completed.

⌒ If it is not renewed within the five years of the IR expiry date, you will be required to do your IRR with a CAA staff examiner (as opposed to an industry examiner authorised by the CAA).

⌒ If it is not renewed within seven years of the IR expiry date, then you lose your ground school credits, and the only way to get your IR back is to retake all of the exams as well as doing another (initial) IR test.

⌒ The IR proficiency check may be combined with a multi- (or single-) engine proficiency check.

⌒ Revalidating/renewing your multi-engine IR in a multi-engined aircraft automatically renews your IR privileges in a single-engined aircraft, providing your single-engine piston class rating is still current.

⌒ Revalidating/renewing your IR in a single-engined aircraft does not renew your IR privileges in a multi-engined aircraft.

⌒ As well as revalidating/renewing your IR you also need to revalidate/renew your single-engine piston class rating and/or your multi-engine piston class rating.

Single-engine piston class rating

A SEP (Land) class rating can be revalidated by flying experience by producing logbook evidence to an appropriately authorised JAR-FCL examiner, before the rating expiry date has passed, of the following flying experience completed within the 12 months preceding the rating expiry date.

12 hours of flight time in SEP or TMG aircraft as appropriate to include;

⌒ **6 hours** as pilot-in-command;

⌒ **12** take-offs and landings;

⌒ A training flight of at least **1 hour's** duration with a flight instructor (A) or class rating instructor (A)* who must countersign the appropriate logbook entry (see full details below).

* The instructor must be authorised in accordance with JAR-FCL to instruct for the JAR-FCL TMG or SEP(Land) rating as appropriate. This training flight may be replaced by any other aeroplane proficiency check or skill test for an instrument, class or type rating (as defined by JAR-FCL) with a JAA qualified examiner, or by a flight test for the issue/ revalidation or renewal of a UK IMC rating

If revalidating by flying experience, and providing the examiner signs the Certificate of Revalidation page within the three months prior to the rating expiry, the validity of the revalidated rating will be calculated from the date of expiry of the preceding rating.

Important note:

If intending to revalidate by flying experience, the Certificate of Revalidation must be signed before the expiry date of the previous rating has passed, otherwise the following SEP rating renewal requirements will apply.

Where licence holders have been unable to renew a SEP (Land) class rating for a period **not exceeding five years** from the date of expiry, they will be required to complete the following requirements:

⌒ The CAA will require no mandatory additional training. Applicants should complete training at their own discretion sufficient to pass the proficiency check.

⌒ Complete the proficiency check with a JAR authorised examiner.

⌒ Pass an oral theoretical knowledge examination conducted by the examiner as part of the proficiency check.

Multi-engine piston class rating

Revalidation of multi-engine piston (Land) class ratings requires a proficiency check with a JAR authorised examiner within the three months preceding the expiry date of the rating*. In addition to this, there is also a minimum flying experience requirement of at least 10 route sectors within the validity of the rating. The experience requirement may be substituted by 1 route sector flown with an authorised examiner that may be undertaken as part of the proficiency check. A route sector is defined as a flight comprising take-off, cruise of not less than 15 minutes, arrival, approach and landing.

* Provided this check is flown within the three month period, the new rating 12 month validity period will run from the date the old one was due to expire.

Where licence holders have been unable to renew a MEP (Land) class rating for a period **not exceeding five years** from the date of expiry, they will be required to complete the following requirements:

⌒ The CAA will require no mandatory additional training. Applicants should complete training at their own discretion sufficient to pass the proficiency check.

⌒ Pass a proficiency check with a JAR authorised examiner.

Carrying passengers

In order to operate an aeroplane or helicopter carrying passengers a pilot must have carried out at least three take-offs and three landings as pilot flying (sole manipulator of the controls) in an aeroplane or helicopter of the same type/class or flight simulator of the aeroplane type/class or helicopter type to be used in the preceding 90 days. In order to carry passengers at night, one of the three take-offs and landings must have been carried out at night, unless a valid JAA/IR is held.

The author is Head of Training and a Director at Professional Air Training Ltd, Bournemouth. The Company specialises in instrument rating training and renewals, especially for the PPL/IR. Anthony has roughly 7,000 hours as a professional flight instructor and is also an examiner for class and instrument ratings, as well as for the initial CPL skill test. This article expresses the personal views of Anthony Mollison for which we sincerely thank him.

3 Obtaining the JAA instrument rating on weekends only

By Christof Edel

A private pilot who intends to fly IFR for personal transport – be it for his own business or for leisure travel – will find it difficult to train in an industry where most IR candidates are young pilots with airline aspirations in full-time training. Both the employed and the self-employed entrepreneurs will find it next to impossible to spare over a month for residential ground school and another month or two for training, so the most likely route is theory by distance learning and then flight training predominantly on week-ends with maybe a few days or a week Mondays to Fridays.

The starting point: a low-time PPL with "ideas above his station"

What follow is my personal account of how I obtained my PPL/IR over the course of a year, along with the things I learnt on the way and that might be useful for anyone who considers taking a similar route. When I started, I was a low-time "weekend pilot" (JAR PPL, 39 years old, 350 hours, IMC & Night, full-time employee, no business related flying) – nothing to write home about. Flying is a useful hobby to me, and I typically do few but long legs – my landings are probably below, but my radio navigation above average for that experience.

Overcoming the detractors – or how to take the plunge

By far the most time wasted getting my IR was not getting started. Apart from time and money, what really held me back for about two years was well-meant advice from three quarters:

1. The "it can't be done" brigade. More than half of the schools or instructors I spoke to initially advised me against doing the IR part-time. Reasons given varied and at times were quite laughable ("nobody passes the IR skill test without having a CPL first"), but the attitude that a PPL/IR just is not done was quite off-putting. The only way to deal with this is to ignore them.

2. The "you won't do it/won't finish, stop wasting my time and save your money" brigade. Many people don't take PPL/IR aspirants seriously, probably because there are so few of them. One way to overcome this is through personal conviction and demonstrating it. Initially, no flight school wanted a serious discussion around the flying course and weekend training. Speaking to the very same people after I had passed the first theory module I was suddenly taken seriously.

3. The "next year will be easier" brigade. There are many changes afoot that might make the PPL/IR more attainable. The theory syllabus has already been reduced by 20% by JAR. ***PPL/IR Europe*** has been lobbying hard for an even more relevant (read slimmer) theory syllabus and competency based training (instead of minimum hours) and this may well happen. There might be a European IMC rating. While all this sounds enticing, I heard all this in 2003, took the advice and waited. Not much happened. I suggest you think of getting the PPL/IR like you would buy a computer: Yes, next years model will be twice as fast at half the price, but if you wait you won't have a computer for that year. Unless there are any definitive changes (and by that I mean firm implementation dates with the legislation already passed) I would just ignore the rumour mill and get on with it. Life is too short, and if the next generation of pilots has it easier, good for them.

Distance learning theory – limited choice

If all you want is an IR with no CPL or instructor rating ever, choices are very limited – only three providers offer IR theory in the UK. If you are thinking about taking the ATPL theory instead "for fun", you probably have a different idea of fun from most other people – it is huge in comparison. The providers are:

- Atlantic Flight Training in Coventry (two modules), www.flyaft.com

- Cranfield Aviation Training (three modules), www.cranfieldaviation.co.uk

- Ground Training Services in Bournemouth (two modules), www.gtserv.co.uk

The courses are structured in "modules" of home study with frequent exercises, both self-assessed and assessed. Each module is then consolidated in on-site ground school, followed by the relevant exams. This structure, combined with the limited exam choice (every two months at Gatwick), gives the following three different approaches one could take:

⌢ Four-month crammer – with AFT (Coventry) or GTS (Bournemouth). These courses have two modules, making it possible to study seven weeks, consolidate one week, do one set of exams and then do it again for module two. With the CAA only setting exams every two months, this is the shortest you can do. Of course, you can give yourself a bit more time by starting studying for module one earlier.

⌢ Six-month course – this is the CAT (Cranfield) model, which uses three modules – learn seven weeks, consolidate one, then test, all that three times. As this adds a trip to Gatwick and a week for consolidation, this is probably not a good option if time off work is an issue.

⌢ Eight-month course – again with AFT or GTS, but taking longer for each module. Anything slower could of course also work, but is probably too slow – it depends on how much you can retain half a year after learning it, then test; all that three times. As this adds a trip to Gatwick and a week for consolidation, this is probably not a good option if time off work is an issue.

The above assumes that you will stick to the school's standard offering. However, these schedules are not set in stone and I would recommend to talk to a provider of your choice about how this could be customised. But expect to pay a bit more in that case, e.g., for 1:1 tuition instead of attending a scheduled course. More recently, I heard of a group of PPL/IR candidates obtaining a customised course at bulk rates.

November – mass and balance issues

Not following my own advice, I did ATPL theory, because I want to do a CPL in order to instruct in a few years time. After looking at the syllabus on the JAA website and after discussing my options with Roger Henshaw at GTS, it quickly became clear that ATPL theory would take less time away from work for consolidations and exams, be more flexible (monthly exams, not every two months). ATPL theory also costs less than separate CPL and IR theory courses for about 20% more content.

A huge, heavy box with the manuals arrived the next day – it was so heavy that I strained my back carrying it home. GTS sets out a detailed suggested schedule which subjects to study when, with regular self assessed exercises, so I got rolling. I found Navigation, Radio-Nav and Meteorology very interesting, although at times a bit irrelevant. For example, I now know how a VOR really works, but am not sure how this helps me to fly better... the syllabus is full of this sort of stuff. On the other hand, some areas are woefully under-represented or not practical enough, e.g., icing, and don't get me started on air law...

Spending most of my evenings and weekends studying, I made good progress, and by mid-December decided to go for the February exams.

January – module 1 consolidation

To minimize time off work, I agreed to replace the first week of the two-week consolidation with 1:1 tuition, which worked well. Roger at GTS was very accommodating; he even rearranged bits of the course to make this possible. However, he also made clear that this would not work for Module 2 – a shame, really, as time off work is quite expensive…

The consolidation course was a good mix of revisions and practice tests with extensive de-briefings. The instructors used the wrong answers given by students to flush out weak areas and cover these in ad hoc revisions rather than just giving the right answer – definitely superior to a question bank. This experience has actually changed my opinion on the consolidations – while I still think they should not be mandatory, they were definitely valuable. I would probably buy one week only, not four…

February - theory exams

The actual exams were as you would expect - sit in a room and mark A, B, C or D for a few hours. The only difference from PPL or IMC exams are a) the location b) the cost and c) the time it takes to score them (three weeks until you know if you have passed). Each of the three is beyond my comprehension… at least I live close enough to Gatwick to make it home each day.

The importance of being earnest

With the first seven exams passed, I went back to talking to schools about the course. I did that with a fair degree of apprehension – I still remembered the negative attitudes I encountered earlier – and found everything completely transformed. After uttering the magic words "I have just passed my Module 1 ATPL Exams" the scepticism disappeared and all instructors I spoke to took the time to discuss options and timeframes – even the ones that fobbed me off two years earlier. I signed up with Stapleford Flight Centre, as they had a good offer and were more than an hour's drive closer than any other IR school.

Fitting in at an ATPL school

Stapleford is geared towards training modular ATPL students, from PPL through CPL, ME and IR with an operation to match. Not all of these students are full-time, especially on the PPL side, but most CPL and IR training takes place during the week and is multi-engine on DA42s or Senecas. While this means that aircraft availability for single-engine IR training is good on week-ends, choice of instructors is a bit limited. But this was quickly sorted – agreeing to different instructors in the simulator and in the air made it a bit easier to fit in, and neither aircraft nor instructor availability was ever a problem. Planning two sorties per weekend should allow me to finish training around August (50 days x 2 sorties at 1 hr 20 on average = 66 hours, leaving room for cancellations).

To get started, we scheduled two simulator slots per weekend.

March and April - boring holes into a virtual sky

The first session was familiarization with the simulator to get used to its control forces – surprisingly realistic – and to establish my present instrument flying skills. Climbs, descents, turns in all variations and combinations, then an NDB track and hold and a final ILS, which all went well except that I crashed the sim on landing, done. The next few sessions were dedicated to a take-off, various NDB hold entries followed by some precision and non-precision approaches at all airfields that I could conceivably fly to on the test. All that took eight hours and was more of a consolidation of previous flying to IR standards and not very challenging for an IMC rated pilot. The lower minima and the requirement of a "stabilized approach" were – at least in the simulator, more on that later – easily met.

Next were airways and skill test profiles, with a take-off at Cranfield, departure to Daventry, airway, STAR or direct to a destination, ILS, go-around and IFR outside controlled airspace to Cranfield, finished off with an NDB hold and a NDB approach to land. For a twin, this would be followed by asymmetric go-around and an asymmetric NDB approach to land, but flying single-engine I could skip that part. This is when the first differences between IMC and IR skill levels emerged, and my weaknesses started showing: ATC liaison, checklist discipline and a lot of safety-related cross checking. There is no tolerance for sloppiness, and many practices are trained that you won't find in CAP 413, e.g., when "cleared for the NDB approach" responding "cleared for the NDB approach, descending 1,650 ft, QNH 998 set" to help catching the two most dangerous things you could do at this stage – descending to the wrong platform altitude or with the wrong QNH set.

Also, the requirement is to use the checklist in flight for all checks, and this together with relatively high workload on departure I found quite difficult – the only real IMC departures I ever did before were at Biggin and were very low workload by comparison. Once on the airway, there are old habits to unlearn and new ones to learn, e.g., how to properly set radios at a waypoint to allow you to check that the OBS for the VOR is set correctly and not 10 degrees off.

The CPL experience

After a total of 17 sim hours, we decide it is time to move on to the aircraft, so I booked my first sorties. Glad to be out on a beautiful day rather than in the dark simulator, I was finally going to learn another difference between CPL and PPL flying – the five yard checklist. While my normal checklist does not even include the magnetic compass except for - obviously - using it to check the HSI and noticing in passing that it has not mysteriously disappeared overnight, the CPL version is "Magnetic Compass – no cracks, no apparent leaks, fluid is clear, no discolourations, no bubbles, deviation card present and readable". Similarly, an altimeter check involves twisting the knob in both directions and a check that the needles cross without snagging. After this flight, my instructor pointed me to the course manual, and I spent every evening the next week practising checklists until I could do them in 20 (!) minutes.

Flying for real – a wake-up call

Once in the air, things came apart quickly. Departure and basic instrument flying were ok, but I was really struggling with trim/pitch changes when setting flaps and operating the undercarriage. All my IMC rating training was in a fixed-gear Warrior and approaches were flown clean, and my previous habits in a Saratoga involved dropping the gear in the intermediate approach, so not much to do there. Now the gear comes down shortly before reaching the glideslope, the flaps are set on intercept, and my initial ILS' were stabilized too late. My go-arounds were even worse, with a tendency to lose climb on flap retraction. Also, with the actual aircraft being a lot less stable than the simulator, work overload and poor checklist discipline raised their ugly head again.

Quite sensibly, the next few sorties were reserved to the whole variety of configuration changes, stalls and recoveries in IMC before moving back to approaches, which we flew at Southend. Each flight is concluded with a "VMC only" practice VOR approach at Stapleford, so being based at a non-IFR airfield was not much of a factor.

Disaster strikes – jury service and work abroad

Sometime in January, I got called up for jury service in May - right during the planned theory consolidation for module 2. That was still ok, pushing exams from June into July, when it turned out that I would be on a project in Israel for most of July and August, so all of the sudden I was out of commission for almost two months – with theory running late as well.

I decided to slow down the training rate, holding back on further sim slots and focusing on the aircraft as this is where my weaknesses were. I managed a total of four sorties in June, July and August to keep reasonably current, but the two months were effectively lost. I spent my lonely hotel evenings and weekends abroad revising theory and, after the August consolidation, passed my final theory exams in September.

Racing winter

With the theory completed, I tried to accelerate my training to finish before the weather turned bad. That meant planning four sorties per weekend, two sim sessions and two actual flights. The sim sessions just continued with skill test profiles, while in the aircraft I concentrated on approach consolidation, then two skill test profiles with an airways flight to Southend and another one to Cambridge. Weather at times interfered, with strong winds or cloud at altitude with icing preventing a few sorties, but by end of September I was approaching test readiness. When instructor sickness interfered, Stapleford quickly drafted another instructor to ensure I could keep training – I was truly impressed by their commitment to have me test ready as early as possible.

Test preparation

Before a candidate is allowed to take the test, he/she has to pass an "170A test", in which an instructor satisfies him/herself that the candidate is ready before signing CAA form 170A. I did a mock skill test with an airways flight to Cambridge, hold, ILS and NDB there and return to Stapleford. With two embarrassing screw-ups I got a "borderline pass" and had to do a "remedial training" sortie the following week end, but a skill test was booked for November 8, two weeks hence.

The day before the skill test, I flew the expected route in the simulator, which also brought my total hours to just above 50, the required minimum.

Skill test in November? In a single???

The first test was fairly unambiguously rained off, with the ceiling at Cranfield hovering at 200ft. After a three hour wait for the improvement forecast in the over-optimistic TAF, I finally gave up and the test was re-booked for the following Tuesday. That day, everything looked fine except for strong winds at altitude (30-40kt crosswind component across the hold, surface winds ok), and the examiners at Cranfield cancelled all tests because they have a testing limit of 30kt holding crosswind. Not quite getting the point and to remain current, I decided to fly a few holds over an NDB using the Cranfield tracks, followed by a few approaches at Southend, after which I was glad I did not try a test in these conditions. Even a 55 degree correction on the outbound leg was not enough to make the inbound track in the hold, and once blown through the track it was very hard to get back – while not missing the beacon outright, the ground tracks must have looked interesting. After landing I heard that my test was rebooked for the next morning, which made me feel good again about that silly sortie – at least I was very current.

Finally – the test

Next morning, the weather was fine, with risk of some cloud (icing!) at airways levels and a warm front moving in later, so we set off from Stapleford to Cranfield for the test. Stapleford send a "chaperone" instructor rather than letting me fly to the test alone – presumably to keep me from committing suicide with the plane after a failed test – which is a good thing as it makes the flight to Cranfield a lot more relaxing. The examiner is happy with my weather assessment and off-airways "Plan B" should we encounter icing, and after checking the paperwork and my PLOG we take off to an airways sector to Daventry and then, after leaving the airway and doing some air-work north of Cranfield, back to the field for a hold, an ILS and a NDB approach to land. Apparently, with singles the local examiners prefer this route rather than flying the ILS elsewhere to keep the test times shorter.

Everything in the test was as expected, and I made only a few minor mistakes, so after vacating the runway I hear the words "That was a pass". Almost an anticlimax – after settling in enroute to DTY, I actually enjoyed most of the test. After paying the hefty fees at Cranfield, we flew back to Stapleford into the approaching warm front, with large parts of that flight in IMC – which, funnily enough, was the most time spent in actual IMC during the entire IR course.

So, after just under a year, I am the proud holder of a JAR IR(A) (SE Only). It took me 30 hours in the simulator and 21 hours in an Arrow to be ready for test, which is just above minimum hours. I needed every single hour in the aircraft (six more than minimum), but probably could have done with a lot less in the simulator – after flying every conceivable test route twice we still had time for a trip from Biggin Hill to

Maastricht and back.

Considering that it took a few people I know longer to get their PPL, I think that the flying part is perfectly achievable for an average PPL – the real killer is the theory: few can afford 2.5-3.five weeks of work, either financially or because family holidays take precedence. So, if you can't or don't want to go the American route, give it a go - don't let yourself be deterred by the conventional wisdom, it is perfectly possible.

Single or twin - does it matter?

The rules:

- An IR obtained on a single-engine aircraft is only valid on singles, a multi-engine IR is valid on both single and twins.

- The SE course is five hours shorter. A later upgrade requires five hours training plus a new skill test (without the airways sector).

Training restrictions in singles

- Flying a single in IMC with low ceilings is a personal choice, similar to SE flying at night. While you might have made the choice to accept the risk of an almost inevitable serious crash after an engine failure, the instructors probably haven't.

- Apart from that, "public transport" flight under IFR in singles is only allowed with ceilings above 1,000 ft, and flying schools might stick to that limit or something similar in their rules.

- Icing at FL90, which is a typical flight level to reach on your airways sector, is frequent in spring and autumn and not unheard of in summer, which can restrict flying in the final third of the course.

- Hence, simulator in late winter, flying in spring and finishing late summer when you do airways and the skill test is probably the best plan.

4   Getting an FAA IR

By Peter Holy

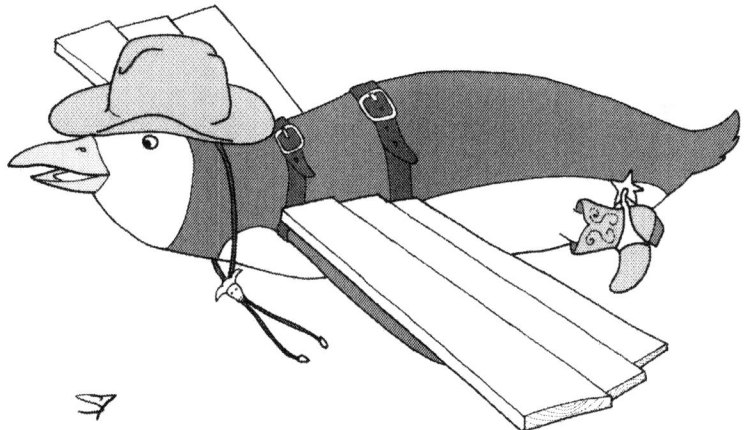

This article is written for a European private pilot who already holds an ICAO PPL and perhaps has some instrument training; for example the UK IMC rating.

I obtained my JAA PPL, Night and IMC rating between 2000 and 2002. One look at the weather made it obvious that an IR would be my objective but it was equally clear from the JAA IR study material (several feet of paper thickness) that this would be a hugely time consuming exercise involving the memorisation of a mountain of largely irrelevant facts. It was years later that I discovered the FAA IR option.

FAA requirements

The FAA IR requires two additional steps: an FAA licence (PPL or CPL), and the aircraft has to be on the N register to get worldwide IFR privileges. So, the process can be separated into three parts:

⌒ FAA PPL;

⌒ FAA IR;

⌒ N registered aircraft.

At this point you need to carefully look at what you want to do in the future.

The simplest case is that you will fly an N-reg aircraft only; the best option then is a standalone FAA PPL and IR. You let any existing European licence/ratings/medical lapse - no point in spending the extra money!

In other cases, where you wish to retain the option to fly for example G-reg aircraft, it may be necessary to retain your existing licence.

UK concession

G-reg pilots have a useful and not well known concession: The UK 2005 ANO Article 21(4) allows you to fly a G-reg, worldwide, on any ICAO PPL, without any paperwork. Other European countries have more onerous processes for flying their respective registrations on an FAA PPL and a UK pilot wishing to rent e.g. F-reg aircraft while in France will want to keep his JAA PPL current. However, the ANO does not allow IFR in controlled airspace which makes an FAA IR somewhat useless on a G-reg.

Standalone or piggyback

The FAA PPL can be done in two ways: a "piggyback" PPL (based on your existing ICAO PPL) or a standalone one (which is completely independent of your existing licences). The latter one is "safer" because the former is based on your existing PPL and medical remaining valid in every way. Also many people forget that a JAA PPL expires every five years! However, historically, many pilots have gone for the piggyback PPL; probably because it used to be possible to get it without visiting the USA. The remainder of this article deals with a standalone FAA PPL.

Requirements

You need an FAA medical, which can be Class 1, 2 or 3. Any of these can be used with an FAA PPL/IR and most people choose Class 3. One known exception is Ireland which requires Class 2 or better for resident pilots. There are several FAA medical examiners living in the UK. The FAA medical tends to be a lot cheaper than the CAA one even though the amount of work is similar.

The FAA PPL training (logbook entry) requirements are set out in FAR 61.103. Apart from 40 hours total time (45 hours for JAA) the only real surprise is the night requirement which includes a 100nm cross country training flight. Most UK PPL holders will need to do this extra night work. The FAA PPL has night privileges as standard; unfortunately for the UK where night flight is usually under IFR, FAR 61.3(e) drops a spanner in the works by requiring an IR. A key concession is that all your existing training, both PPL and instrument, is allowed towards the FAA training requirements. So, you could do it all in a G-reg with a JAA instructor! The only exception, for both the PPL and the IR, is the last three hours within 60 days of the respective check ride which needs to be done with an FAA CFI/CFII instructor for practical reasons: an FAA instructor has to sign you off as ready for the check ride.

Training in an N-reg in the UK

Any instruction in UK airspace requires a JAA instructor rating - unless the instructor doesn't get paid. This is regardless of aircraft registration. However, few FAA instructors also have a JAA instructor rating. The obvious alternatives are to do it outside the UK, or find an instructor who does not charge for the flights. It is unclear whether this has ever been applied to check rides for foreign licences. Various options for UK based FAA check rides were mostly closed down during 2003-2004. A move by the FAA to require all examiners to get permission for work outside the USA didn't help and the supply of examiners in Europe has practically dried up. So, at the time of writing, it's off to the USA... A step by step guide to lengthy but manageable visa/TSA process is here: www. peter2000.co.uk/aviation/faa-pplir/tsa-visa.html.

UK or USA?

Almost every pilot will need additional training to reach the FAA PPL and IR test standards. The need to go to the USA for the check ride dramatically changes the outlook on where to do any additional training.

Most pilots working towards the FAA IR are people with incomes above the UK GA average and will thus live correspondingly busy lives. They prefer to do everything in the UK and slot the training into their life, often in their own aircraft. To cater for this "market", there are some FAA training operations around the UK; usually these take you up to the sign-off stage and then send you to the USA for the check ride. My view is that this is OK for building up any required logbook entries but less good for general competence - unless the school in the USA can offer an aircraft identical to the one you are current on in the UK.

FAA written exams

The FAA written exams are computer based multiple choice and can be sat in several locations around Europe. There are several PC-based question-bank-based software packages which one can use to prepare for the FAA written and oral exams.

I did the standalone FAA PPL in the UK a few years previously. The pre-check ride training involved several hours of flight in a PA28, covering some exercises specific to FAA which do not feature in the JAA PPL. The oral was around one hour of hard questioning; the examiner may well ask about matters which no UK pilot could possibly know from experience (US airspace rules and weather services is a favourite). The check ride was very thorough, under a lot of pressure. At the time I had some 300 hours, the majority flying a TB20 "by the numbers" and it didn't help to have had so little time on the PA28, doing short-field and soft-field takeoffs for example.

N Register

Having the FAA PPL opened the way to placing the aircraft on the N register, which I did in 2006. This process is best done during an annual and best summarised by saying that you must find a maintenance company which has demonstrated experience of doing it with your aircraft type. There are pitfalls which can ground your aircraft for months!

To meet FAA aircraft ownership rules, you need to find a trust company which legally owns your aircraft, with you being the beneficial owner. These range from inexpensive to very expensive depending on what type of trust or corporate structure you wish the aircraft to operate under.

"Life" intervened again to delay the process, but by early 2006 I was ready for my two weeks in the USA for the IR.

I allowed two weeks for this based on previous reports of other UK pilots' experiences; in the end the exercise proved to be a lot harder and two weeks worked out just right. At the time, I had a UK PPL, Night, the UK IMC rating, and a standalone FAA PPL and about 550 hours total time of which about 450 were done, over a period of three years, on the TB20. I had already passed the FAA IR written exam and had all the required logbook requirements except the 250nm cross-country flight with three different instrument approaches. I had about 70 hours instrument time, comprising of about 30 hours of various instructional flights; the remainder being real instrument time in actual IMC without the use of the autopilot.

The FAA IR written exam had been done in the UK. Having done this first was essential and it would have been impossible to do the IR in the two weeks otherwise.

The other preparation I had done back home involved watching the rather tedious King video training material. This is worth sitting through but I did wonder just how many times Martha King was going to explain what a VOR was... I think this is best watched shortly before the exam.

Choosing a US school

In brief, to get the M1 visa, one needs an I20 form which can be issued only by a school in a scheme called SEVIS and only Part 141 schools are members. This excludes most of the small schools in the USA which are Part 61 only.

After several dead ends (which included getting TSA clearance for a Part 61 school, only to discover I would never get the visa!), I settled on Chandler Air Service at Phoenix, Arizona. The location was preferred for its excellent weather which would minimise the risk of not getting finished in the time available.

Arizona

The immigration officer at Phoenix carefully checked my TSA and visa paperwork.

I never adjusted to the local time, going to bed 7pm and getting up 3am. This bizarre approach suits the training quite well as the first lesson often starts 07:30, and there was nothing much to do in the evenings. The neighbourhood is mostly car parts shops and snack shops selling rubbish food. Perhaps unexpectedly, there was no social scene at the school - another good reason for going to bed at 7pm. This two-week visit was planned to be a 100% "get your head down and get it done" project. This tactic also avoids the seven-hour jet lag upon return to the UK which would otherwise take a week to fully get over.

Chandler Air Service

Chandler Air Service is based at the Chandler Municipal Airport (KCHD). They have about 25 aeroplanes and do a lot of aerobatic training alongside the PPL and IR. The staff were really pleasant and the instructors were very competent.

Training aircraft

The aeroplanes are mostly PA28 Warriors of varying ages. The utilisation was very high, with anything up to six one-hour flights every day the maintenance book was full of 100-hour checks so they received frequent maintenance.

The training aircraft were basic but everything in the panel worked - except the autopilot (marked "INOP") on the one I was flying. No GPS was fitted so no GPS was taught; just the traditional VOR/DME and lots and lots of it, mostly on partial panel. The converse is true: if GPS is fitted you will have to learn all about it. There were no more NDB procedures taught because they are being phased out so they are no longer in the syllabus - although, apparently, if the aircraft used for the check ride carries an ADF the examiner might give you an NDB approach. The lack of GPS – my deliberate choice - means you don't learn GPS approaches, but that hardly matters since they are almost nonexistent in Europe. It's probably a good thing for this purpose because learning to use an IFR GPS correctly is a job for a few more days, and one can learn GPS approaches closer to home, if they are ever needed. Also, the approach sequencing is highly GPS unit specific.

The first two days were really hard. I could not understand much of the rapid and often heavily accented radio traffic, and got confused by the fact that the actual flights were all done under VFR but I was doing the IFR radio calls to the instructor only who pretended to be the controller, and he was giving me IFR clearances, vectors, etc. After day three I was starting to get the hang of the context. All flying was under the hood, which came on immediately after takeoff. About half the training, and most of the check ride including unusual attitude recoveries, was flown on partial panel.

Ground school was about $40/hour and I had about five hours.

Training area

The training area was very small; within about 30 x 20 miles, which made the flying very intensive. Every flight was packed from takeoff to landing, with barely a minute's rest. There was no "cruise segment". There was just enough time to trim the aeroplane for level flight before intercepting the first VOR radial; the next radial came up two minutes later and the VOR approach three minutes after that. This is quite unlike most real flying because one normally has time to think and plan. The short distances, if combined with random vectors from the "pretend-ATC" instructor, also mess up any situational awareness which you think you had. A pilot with 500 hours, current, including a fair bit of UK IFR, should already know how to do the individual flying bits, but this intensity is something else. It's easy to end up on the wrong side of some radial because you shot through it without noticing. The training includes a procedure where you need to be able to look at two VOR (CDI) displays and immediately tell where you are relative to the two radials. This is a neat trick but in my view close to worthless for real IFR flying because it works over about 160 degrees so you could end up with an intercept that is uselessly far away. One needs a bit more than that for decent situational awareness. A proper position fix requires a VOR/VOR or VOR/DME fix but this of course takes longer...

Flight Training

Every approach was flown to minima. Upon reaching the decision height you would announce "decision height" and the instructor or examiner would tell you if you were going to land or go missed. As I expected having done a fair bit of ILS back home, I flew good ILS approaches. Unexpectedly I also flew reasonably good partial panel (DI and AI covered up) VOR approaches and holds, using timed turns only. As always, getting the plane trimmed makes everything much easier, but this is easier said than done if there is a lot of thermal turbulence (common in Arizona after the early morning) or when the next radial to intercept comes up 20 seconds after you have reached top of climb... In fact, flying approaches was the easy part. The hard part was intercepting one radial, then another one a few miles later, then getting vectored about five times in rapid sequence, then (when the vectoring has made you lose all situational awareness) being asked to intercept another radial. They expect you to be able to take one look at the two CDIs and know right away where you are and which way to turn. It's doable but having to do radio calls as well really raises the workload.

A few more days later, it became a bit easier. I was getting better organised. However I was still making a number of mistakes on every flight - mostly little ones, to do with radio calls and nothing dangerous flying-wise. In fact, I would say that from the start and throughout the training my flying was safe. Even the partial panel stuff with timed turns was OK. I just did not work fast enough...

The PA28-161, with its low wing loading, is amazingly unstable (for a "tourer") in the thermal turbulence, and would tip into a 45 degree bank and change heading by about 30 degrees in much less time than it takes to write down a clearance. This drastically increased the workload, to the point where I was sometimes unable to do anything else even when flying straight and level. The other little thing I noticed, having been flying behind the TB20 constant speed prop for a few years, is just how much harder a fixed pitch prop aircraft is in updraughts and downdraughts: you get an updraught, you have to point the nose down, and the faster airflow causes the engine to rev up, so pulling back on the power is a lot more essential than with a CS prop. I had never realised this huge benefit of a CS prop: superior pitch stability. Flying early in the day, before the thermals build up, is the key, but I would not like to fly there at all in the summer!

The 250nm cross-country was done after the first week. We flew IFR down to Tucson and then to Nogales; a tiny airfield close to the Mexican border but the Customs presence gives it the "Nogales International" title.

The flight was uneventful and due to the generous airway MEAs most of it was done around 10,000 feet. The radio work on this flight was entirely for real as it was flown under an IFR flight plan.

America is truly the land of aviation freedom. There are hard-runway airfields everywhere, and most of them have instrument approaches. There are even many air parks (residential communities with an airfield attached) with ILS or GPS approaches! This is quite unlike anywhere in Europe. All the charts, en-route, terminal and instrument approach, are free. In Europe, while some countries make their instrument approach and terminal charts freely available online, in practice it is usually necessary to buy a subscription for these and en-route charts from a commercial provider.

Planning for the check ride

Two days before the check ride I flew with an examiner (not the one I was finally to have), for a mock check ride. He was relatively outspoken but I liked him; he was very fair and he made good points and made them well. Again I made a few mistakes but nothing major.

The day before the check ride, I met the final examiner who gave me an assignment to plan, for the flight early the following morning. This was an airways flight of about 300 miles to an airfield in New Mexico. The job was to plan the flight back at the hotel, as an IFR flight obviously, taking into account the various rules on the chart and the approach plates, etc. It is different to European airways flight planning and is much easier; for example there are no mandatory Standard Route Documents so no need to plug away at the CFMU website to get a valid Eurocontrol flight plan. I was also to fill in a real flight plan form - but not actually file it because as far as ATC was concerned all this training was under VFR. It took a few hours to do the planning. One has to work out the altitudes (no "flight levels" below 18,000 feet in the USA) and get the winds aloft along the route. Traditionally this is done with a phone call to 1-800-WX-BRIEF and unless you are lucky the forecaster will talk so fast you initially won't catch much of it. There is also a way to get the same data off the web but I never found it. So I used the GFS data which we use in Europe, mainly for longer range forecasts, and Avbrief for TAFs and METARs.

The FAA allows the use of any method of working out the wind corrected plog, so no need for the circular slide rule so much loved by European aviation traditionalists. The slide rule is not required in any of the FAA written exams either; they just don't permit anything with a "memory" unless the test supervisor can clear the memory and verify that it has been cleared. The flight plan TAS, for each altitude, comes from the PA28-161 POH, from the "best power" setting, the OAT and the altitude, for 65% power. Given the crude leaning procedure to get what one thinks is 65% power and its corresponding fuel flow, this calculation (common in flying schools everywhere) needs to be done with generous fuel margins!! There isn't the instrumentation in the aircraft to meter fuel accurately. Nor is one going to get the planned TAS. During the check ride, the planned flight is started but isn't completed (it would be much too long).

Test day

The following morning I turned up with a load of weather printouts and the flight plan. Luckily I had a portable inkjet printer; the Canon IP90, and I used it to print out approach plates, from Jeppview, in a familiar format throughout the two weeks. However, this is far from essential as in the USA the free plates are perfectly OK.

I had to turn up with the right documents for myself: a proof of picture (passport) and a separate proof of address (this was a problem; a UK utility bill would be fine but luckily I had some TSA paperwork showing my address) with neither being a pilot-related document. Plus the medical. All in original, no copies. I also had to retrieve the maintenance documents and the flight manual from the aircraft, and "prove" to the examiner that the aircraft was airworthy.

If you are adding your IR rating to an FAA PPL certificate issued under FAR 61.75 (a "piggyback" licence issued on the basis of your JAA/UK licence) then you must also have a current "Verification of Authenticity of Foreign License" letter from the FAA. You will have needed to get one of these when you got your 61.75 licence, but they are only valid for six months. If you don't have a current one you will not be allowed to take your check ride and it's not possible to get one in less than about three weeks so you will have had a wasted journey!

There is a strong preference in the training to phone the 1-800-WX-BRIEF weather service, although I understand most "real" pilots do use internet weather. WX-BRIEF came back with almost the same winds and temperatures aloft as I had in the GFS data; unsurprising since the US forecasts come from GFS anyway. A slight complication was that there was quite a lot of "weather" in the area (a warm front) and there was no data available for the destination so one had to take a wider view of the area.

The examiner was an old chap who looked really laid back but in reality he was as sharp as they come. He started by examining my flight planning. Apart from trivial points, he could not fault it. As he was going through this, he would ask various related questions - just like a tax inspector. He also went through the standard regulatory items like required documents on the pilot and in the aircraft, lost comms procedures (picking a point along the route where a radio failure occurs, and asking where you will go from there both laterally and vertically all the way to destination), required aircraft maintenance, etc. He was very thorough. I knew nearly all of it and he did not catch me out on anything of substance. He also explained a lot of stuff, which was good. I understand the official FAA position is that the candidate should learn something from every examination. The oral lasted about two hours and was a good learning experience.

The flight test

The examiner started off very quiet and no doubt he planned to stay that way. I made various errors in the radio calls; the usual confusion as to who to talk to for real or not for real. So he soon started reminding me of missed radio calls. He got really going when I wasn't doing things fast enough due to pressure. But in retrospect I did all the actual flying well, with the worst thing being the glide slope going to just half scale (on the safe side) at the 200 feet DH, which is OK. This was followed by "Runway visual, land" instruction at the DA so we did a low approach and a missed.

Items like a fully developed stall, partial panel, while holding a heading and altitude, I did perfectly, and same with all unusual attitude recoveries. On the return flight, he progressively failed instruments and in the end I was flying a partial panel VOR approach, with just the TC, the compass at the top, and one VOR receiver which had to be rapidly switched (and retuned) between two VORs; one to track and the other for the crosscuts. This verges on the ridiculous and if you can do this you can probably do anything. I did it OK in terms of overall accuracy but was unable to do much else like radio calls. The check-ride contained just about everything covered in the training, ending with a partial-panel timed-turns hold, to a VOR approach terminating with a right-hand circle to land.

I suspect that if I had actually messed up badly, e.g. turned the wrong way somewhere, he would have failed me. One can read the IR Practical Test Standards (PTS) booklet (worth reading) but basically you will fail if you do something where the examiner has to take the controls. You will probably also fail if you make a gross navigation error, or mess up some instrument approach. I doubt they will fail you for occasionally not doing the radio when under pressure. This suggests that if you can do all the flying and do it safely and reasonably accurately then you should pass.

One is expected to hold altitude to within 100 feet. In turbulence this often cannot be achieved; what they are looking for is an immediate detection of the deviation and a corrective action taken.

The flying was much too intense to enjoy and two flights per day was the maximum I could take. A lot of people go to fly in the USA hoping for a holiday and "picking up an IR" while they are at it; this is not going to be the case! It was readily apparent that the criticism of the FAA IR, widespread in the UK aviation scene, is mostly rubbish written by people who have never actually done it.

The IR check ride also counts as a BFR (biennial flight review) for the FAA PPL so that now runs for two more years also.

Total cost of the training was £2,400. On top of this were the airline flights, two weeks' accommodation, and food. Plus perhaps a week of cumulative UK time spent pushing pieces of paper and hanging around the US Embassy.

Would I recommend this school? If you want a hard, thorough but basic IR done at a school which is very straight, honest and makes sure you do it right, then certainly yes. If you want to fly a nice aircraft with a glass cockpit, there are schools that fly those but allow an extra week to learn the avionics and the extra items which you will get tested on; however, due to the variations between the different kinds of these relatively advanced avionics, it will be a waste of money unless you fly with similar equipment back home. I would also avoid the summer in Arizona; it gets extremely hot and the thermals will make flying hard.

On reflection, a UK IMC rated pilot who has had a good instructor back in the UK, with good IFR currency (probably an aircraft owner) and with good technical knowledge should already be able to do most of what is required, and two weeks of additional training should be enough. He will still find it very hard to work at the required speed though, and there are enough differences between the UK and the USA to use up several days' training. Doing 150 hours a year I had more currency than most UK private pilots but I still found it very hard.

It's hard to guess how much work it would have been for a plain PPL with no instrument experience. Probably a good two months and that assumes one has passed the written exam already and knows the theory. The UK IMC rating is an excellent preparation for the FAA IR because it should give you about 60% of the theory and most of what is involved in actual IFR flight. The IR then involves a significant improvement in one's standard of flying and this is much harder than one would expect.

The IR was the hardest thing, flying-wise, that I have ever done - by far. Finishing it was a huge relief. Now, for the first time in two years, I can pick up a normal book or a magazine and read it, without feeling guilty that I should really be reading the FAR/AIM or the ASA training guide.

Was it worth doing? The FAA IR route avoids the huge ground study of the JAA IR but introduces several additional complications, the chief ones being the need to find time to visit the USA and the need to arrange access to an N-registered aircraft to get the IFR privileges. For me, with good access to a suitable aircraft, the clear answer is YES. The FAA IR process is a lot easier to slot into one's life than the JAA ground material which, for most people with a "life", will need a year or two of dedicated study. However, for someone who needs full IFR privileges in a European-registration aircraft, for example someone renting from flying clubs, the JAA IR is the only option.

After the IR?

On the last day I sat and passed the FAA commercial pilot written exam, and a year later completed the CPL in the UK. The FAA CPL is all-VFR and is a very worthwhile exercise for the additional training in aircraft handling. The theory is mostly of aircraft technical nature and is relevant to private flying. An FAA CPL has little commercial use in Europe though.

Aircraft owners

It would be highly desirable to do it all in one's own aircraft. Currency on type is what it's all about and this training should be fully utilised. It is possible but difficult to do all this in the UK; the alternative is to find an identical aircraft in USA.

The number of pilots willing to go through the considerable hassle of doing the FAA PPL/IR, placing the aircraft on the N register, etc, highlights how poorly conceived the European pilot licensing regime really is.

Flying in Europe

How different is flying in Europe? In all flight training, there are gaps between the training and what a pilot really needs to know to go places. In PPL training, this knowledge gap is such that most PPLs feel unable to do anything useful. When it comes to the IR, there are significant gaps on the operational side of things; for example, the development of a route acceptable to Eurocontrol ranges from nontrivial to very difficult and this isn't taught in any IR (FAA or JAA). The flying itself is usually easy; European IFR is largely an RNAV point to point navigation exercise with a BRNAV GPS, terminating with an instrument approach which is usually radar vectored. This, or the more complicated variants where e.g. a SID/STAR has to be flown using a series of navaids, isn't going to cause any problems to an FAA IR holder.

Many small details are different of course: the radio, and many little procedural items. It would be highly advisable for any new IR holder (FAA or JAA) to fly with an experienced pilot before venturing out on their own around Europe.

The real long-term challenge for an IR holder is currency. This requires good access to an aircraft equipped to a high standard, and an appropriate budget.

5 Beyond the PPL/IR: an overview of recurrent and advanced training

By Vasa Babic

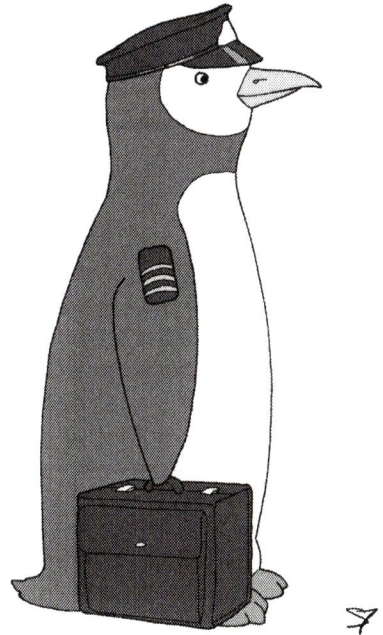

Getting an instrument rating is one of the biggest steps in the flight training hierarchy, in terms of the learning it requires and the capabilities it makes available. However, beyond the initial IR, there is both a need for practical learning on how to operate in the IFR environment and a continuing effort to maintain currency, in particular given the pace of change in airspace, regulations, procedures and avionics.

This article is about the options a PPL/IR pilot has for further training beyond the initial instrument rating and its annual JAA revalidation or FAA Biennial Flight Review (BFR). Why might these be interesting? I have found a number of motivations:

- *Currency:* offers alternative means of keeping current and improving skills;

- *Cost:* some training options can be relatively inexpensive, especially for the pilot whose marginal cost of flying is high because they rent an airplane or operate a high-performance type;

- *Intrinsic interest:* training can be fun and worthwhile in of itself;

⌒ *Increased capabilities:* training can help extend the scope of flying you can undertake, and perhaps defray some cost or insure you against future regulatory challenges;

⌒ *Incremental achievement:* many post-IR training options are attainable in quite manageable steps and require little or no renewal or currency – it's a nice upwards 'ratchet' that accumulates over the years;

⌒ *Safety:* most importantly, training has safety benefits which apply well beyond the minimum needed to earn and maintain the pilot privileges you use.

I have done most of the FAA fixed-wing options and dabbled in some of the JAA professional training, so the emphasis here is on 'advanced' airplane training, which I think is most relevant to a PPL/IR, rather than 'parallel' alternatives like aerobatics, tail draggers, helicopters etc. It is also very much an overview, intended to provide some ideas and suggestions rather than a detailed analysis of courses and requirements. In particular, when it comes to commercial and instructor licences, I do not aim to give an exhaustive précis of LASORS and FAR 61&91. Please treat the article as a pointer to these authoritative sources. References can be found at the end of the chapter.

1. Standard recurrent training

Everyone is familiar with the JAA 12-month revalidation[1] or the FAA requirements for the BFR and 6-month instrument currency[2]. Personally I find the JAA approach to be a reasonable minimum, but a fairly rigid and formulaic one – when I used to do these regularly in a Seneca at Bournemouth, I got the feeling the aircraft knew its own way around the standard training routes and I certainly knew the tracks, navaids, idents and procedures from memory. I tend to prefer the more modern "scenario" and "line orientated" training methods, but there's no question that the JAA revalidation is a solid foundation for IFR flight. The FAA approach is less formally demanding, but places the demand on pilots (and BFR instructors) to adapt training to their personal requirements – used wisely, this flexibility should increase, rather than minimise, the training a pilot does.

2. Other recurrent training

There are three main options for recurrent training beyond the basic requirements of your IR and license:

Ad hoc training at a flight school or with an instructor on your own airplane

Some schools and instructors are a bit bewildered by someone electing to train when they don't have to. In terms of flight schools, I would prefer a commercial FTO, whose instructors are experienced professional pilots, but you need to find one that's flexible and willing to serve an ad hoc PPL/IR customer who is not a full-time airline cadet. For instruction on one's own airplane, the UK IRE/CRE list in the **PPL/IR Europe**'s website 'Getting a Rating'[3] section is a good start.

Another option, as modern aircraft become increasingly available at flight schools, is to try training on new designs like the Cirrus SR20 or Diamond DA42, or on a familiar type fitted with Garmin G1000 or Avidyne avionics. Personally, after hundreds of hours in tired, old club trainers, I have found my interest in small piston aircraft rejuvenated by flying some of the new types; in its 2006 variant, even the humble C172 feels completely transformed.

Ad hoc dual flight instruction is perhaps most useful for a pilot who flies less than they find ideal for currency. For a PPL/IR flying regularly, an hour or two of dual is always useful, but may be somewhat limiting, given the familiarity of routes and approaches near one's home base, and the narrow set of failures which can be simulated in-flight.

Ad hoc training on FNPT2 simulators

I think that the latest generation of FNPT2 simulators[4] are the most under-used resource in GA recurrent training. The list of simulator training advantages, especially for the pilot who is current in normal aircraft operations, is a very long one: cost per hour, intensity of useful training per hour, ability to simulate many kinds of failure, ability to practice distant or inaccessible procedures etc. For twin pilots, the advantages are particularly compelling, given the limited range of engine failures that can be safely simulated in an aircraft (and the further limitations careful engine management may impose).

A couple of years ago I went to BCFT at Bournemouth and developed this 5hr ME-IR recurrency course to brush-up after a lull in my flying:

Session 1   1.5hrs: JAA IR test format, to get up to speed with the Sim

Session 2   1.5hrs: JAA IR test format but with lots of unexpected extras (e.g. engine failure immediately after take-off , zero-zero takeoff and landing, various system failures)

Session 3   2hrs: LOFT (Line-Orientated Flight Training)-style scenario[5] involving a difficult route, unplanned diversion, multiple failures etc.

I consider this the minimum annual training I need to safely use my FAA IR privileges in full, complemented by a VFR check (ideally staggered by six months) to keep my JAA MEPL-IR current. Having both done an initial 5-day training course for my Cessna 421C on a type-specific FTD (Flight Training Device) and flown generic FNPT2 Sims, I think that, as long as you are current on your airplane and familiar with its systems and emergency procedures, a generic simulator of the appropriate SEPL or MEPL class will have 80-90% of the value of a type-specific one, for just about any piston airplane.

The advantages of simulator training are increasing as more pilots transition to advanced avionics like the Garmin G1000, and as the need for GPS approach and PRNAV procedure training becomes more prevalent.

One option I suggest would be to find a willing school with a GNSx30-equipped FNPT2 and a full European IFR database and to create a ~5hr course which combines your IR renewal with a GPS approach and PRNAV training endorsement[6]. This could consist of:

A. Ground study

⌒ Read the Garmin GNSx30 series manuals and training materials if required[7];

⌒ Study the Jeppesen Instrument Procedures Guide book on GPS approaches if required[8];

⌒ Read all of Jens Gjerlev's excellent and concise book 'Instrument Flight Procedures'[9], (should only be a few hours reading).

B. FNPT2 training

Agree a syllabus with your instructor to cover your requirements, which might include:

⌒ 1.5hrs of JAA IR renewal using overlay procedures on the Garmin GNSx30

⌒ 1.5hrs practising pure GPS approaches (e.g. the UK trial ones)

⌒ 2.0hrs practising RNAV procedures and approaches (e.g. at LHAM Schiphol, which has a plethora to choose from), ideally covering all of TGL10.5 (see reference 6)

If satisfactorily completed, your instructor should be willing to endorse your logbook accordingly. A pilot with less GPS experience could focus on normal flying in this kind of course, whilst a more expert GNSx30 user could include various aircraft and avionics failures (e.g. GPS loss of integrity and reversion to non-RNAV procedures).

Formal simulator courses at US schools

The US has a strong culture of GA recurrent training, supported by insurance requirements and the size of the GA aircraft fleet. A number of simulator schools[10] offer 4-6 day initial courses and 2-3 day refresher courses on specific advanced piston and light turbine aircraft types. The format of each day is usually 4hrs of ground school on systems and performance, and 2-3hrs training in a full-visual FTD, built from an actual aircraft cockpit. Some also offer 2-day "generic" multi-engine or single-engine IFR refreshers.

These courses are not cheap, they work out at US$600-800 per day. Generally, it is more economical if two people do a course together and share an instructor, or if you are a regular with the school and eligible for loyalty discounts. The quality of service and facilities is very high – they are designed for business people with their own airplanes, rather than airline cadets on a tight budget. You do not need TSA/AFSP approval or a visa, and some of the locations can be combined with a family holiday .

On balance, I would recommend the initial courses most strongly for pilots making a major transition towards more complex piston aircraft . You are really combining two types of learning: differences training for a specific type and recurrent training on that type . A pilot with limited multi-engine time moving up to an Aerostar, C340, C421, Navajo or B60 Duke may find an initial course essential, whilst an experienced Seneca pilot moving to a Baron probably wouldn't.

For a European pilot who has to travel to the US, I think the 2-3 day type-specific recurrent courses are not as efficient as the generic FNPT2 training described above, unless you either fly a light turboprop or fly an advanced piston type infrequently enough to merit formal brush-up training on its systems and operation. For example, in September 2006, I planned a trip to Arizona to do a Simcom refresher on the 421C. However, with 150hrs on type in the prior 12 months, I did not feel the need for many classroom hours on the 421 and chose instead to do a Beech King Air B200 initial course. This was an enjoyable way of both learning about turbine aircraft and getting recurrent IFR training (but with the disadvantage that the B200's single-engine performance bears no resemblance to a piston twin). Since most of the training in this article is 'elective', nothing stops you from choosing courses you find fun and interesting.

In summary, the four US schools listed in reference 10, below, offer great training options; essential ones for transitioning to some complex aircraft types, and non-essential ones which might be attractive given a pilot's personal inclination, travel schedule and overall currency. For FAA certificate holders, they can also meet IPC, BFR and high altitude endorsement requirements. Have a browse of the websites listed, and call the schools if you are interested. I found Simcom perfectly willing to tailor courses and schedules to one's individual preference, if, for example, you had a free day on a business trip and simply wanted to spend the maximum time in the FTD practising engine failures after take-off in your twin type.

3. Commercial pilot training

FAA commercial pilot certificate

For an experienced FAA private pilot, the requirements to upgrade to a commercial certificate are quite modest. There is a single written test which covers the same ground as the private test, with additional material on commercial privileges and currency[12]. There are some detailed flight experience requirements, most of which a PPL/IR will already meet[13].

Separate check rides are needed for single-engine and multi-engine commercial privileges. My advice is to get whichever is easiest for you to earn the initial commercial certificate, and add-on the other at a later time if you want. The multi-engine commercial check ride can be combined with an initial multi-engine IFR one – there is no real difference except some tighter tolerances, and it is a relatively "easy win" if you can get the extra study for the written test done. The single-engine commercial check ride is similar to the private pilot one, with tighter tolerances and some additional manoeuvres (chandelles, lazy 8s, turns around a point). If you can generally fly to the FAA Practical Test Standard (PTS), you may only need a few dual hours to practice the manoeuvres.

Of course, you may never use the commercial privileges, so why bother? There is no reason in particular, but a number of items might make it worthwhile relative to the not-excessive cost and effort:

⌒ Sharpen-up your VFR and general handling skills;

⌒ Meet the BFR requirements by passing a check ride;

⌒ Earn the distinction of a commercial certificate, valid for your life-time;

⌒ Potentially, gain some safeguards against more restrictive European requirements in the future: an ICAO CPL currently exempts you from many of the training and ground study requirements needed for an initial JAA CPL;

⌒ For $30-40 an hour more, you could do the single-engine training on a G1000-equipped C172 and thus complete G1000 conversion at the same time.

FAA ATP

For the determined FAA pilot with 1500hrs or more (I hope to be there in a few years!) the ATP is also a fairly attainable step. It is still only one written exam, albeit with a much heftier syllabus. The check rides are ME/SE class specific, to quite demanding tolerances, and, unlike the commercial PTS, include IFR procedures. The FAA ATP offers some good short-cuts to the frozen JAA ATPL (including exemption from theory course classroom attendance) but not to the 500hrs multi-crew time needed to 'un-freeze' it.

Given that 'grandfather rights' tend to be respected when new regulations are introduced, the FAA ATP is also the ultimate step for the Foreign Registered Aircraft (FRA) operator who fears being forced into the EASA licensing system or fears that, at some future time, the most advanced airspace and GA aircraft types may become inaccessible to the plain PPL.

JAA CPL(A)

The JAA CPL(A) flight training is a fraction of the cost of a JAA IR – it is in the region of £5,000 for 25 single-engine hours (five of which have to be on a complex aircraft, typically the PA28R) or merely 'training as required' for holders of an ICAO CPL[14].

The JAA CPL Theory[15] is something of an anomaly. It's probably the least studied JAR-FCL course. If you already have a JAA IR, then a lot of the material will be familiar, but you still need to take eight of the nine CPL papers (you are exempt Human Performance). If you don't have a JAA IR, then the full ATPL distance learning ground school makes much more sense, because it gives you more privileges then the combination of CPL and IR theory, for less study time, cost and fewer exam papers to sit[16]. However, if you hold an FAA CPL/IR, you are exempt the compulsory JAA classroom training for the CPL and IR exams, but not the ATPL ones.

I have recently started studying for the JAA ATPLs. Compared to the FAA theory, the actual content and exams do not seem more difficult, but the volume of both is greater and there is the infuriating requirement for classroom attendance. The whole FAA vs. JAA debate is beyond the scope of this article, but, for what it's worth, I personally feel the regulatory tide is shifting in favour of sticking to the JAA system, when you combine the possibility of EASA easing some training regulations and increasing the restrictions on FRA based in Europe with the visa and TSA bureaucracy needed for training in the US.

The JAA CPL is probably the most demanding of the 'elective' courses covered in this article. It is more of a long-term project than a weekend recurrent training option. However, training which seems dauntingly expensive and time-consuming at first, can become quite attainable in practice, simply by chipping away at the requirements one step at a time.

4. Instructor training

This section will not describe how to become a fully-fledged flight instructor from scratch; plenty of US and European school websites outline such courses in great detail. What I thought *PPL/IR Europe* members might find interesting are some options for instructor qualifications that may be surprisingly attainable. Even more surprisingly, the most attainable are JAR-FCL qualifications rather than FAA ones!

Why get an instructor qualification when most of us struggle to fly enough, let alone instruct? Firstly, the training can be effective purely for major 'de-rusting,' skills enhancement and confidence-building. Secondly, you can use instructor privileges to give recurrent training, legally and safely, to a pilot you share a trip with, both of you logging the flight time and learning from what might otherwise have been a routine 'bimble'. Thirdly, instructor training can have some useful synergistic benefits; for example, I passed my FAA instrument instructor check ride on a G1000-equipped C172, teaching GPS procedures and approaches, which neatly, I think, makes me compliant with the differences training requirement both for the G1000 and for flying GPS IAPs in Europe. Additionally, some instructor privileges are not hard to maintain, even if you do not do a lot of teaching. The FAA requires a 24 month renewal, which can be done on-line, and the JAA class rating instructor requires only some modest training every three years.

JAA class rating instructor (CRI) MEPL and SEPL[17] [18]

These two JAA qualifications are somewhat obscure, but very useful and attainable. You do not need a JAA CPL, you do not need to pass the JAA CPL Theory and you do not need a Class 1 medical. The CRI courses require a fair amount of ground school (25-30hrs) but only a modest minimum amount of flight training (5hrs CRI-MEPL, 3hrs CRI-SEPL). The cost is about £2500-£3300 for the CRI-MEPL and only £1200 for the CRI-SEPL, plus a skills test with a JAA flight instructor examiner.

As a CRI, you can not teach *ab initio* students, but you can provide differences, recurrent and renewal/revalidation training. You can also teach students for the initial class rating, but this must be through an approved course at a JAA flight training organisation. A PPL CRI may not receive any valuable consideration for instructing.

I did the CRI-MEPL at BCFT in May 2006 and found it one of the best courses I have done. The ground school has two elements: the theory of learning and training, a 'foundation' for any FI rating, and the theory specific to the class rating. I initially thought the learning theory was a bit waffly and abstract, but it actually turned out to be quite interesting, and even relevant to professional work outside of aviation. The multi-engine theory covered the same topics as the initial MEPL class rating in much greater depth. I had 800hrs of twin time at this point, and it felt very worthwhile to try and master multi-engine theory from a senior ground instructor of vast experience.

The flight training is very structured, and it focuses on teaching the JAA multi-engine piston class rating. It is broken down into five lessons, and for each you are taught exactly how to give a detailed ground briefing and how to conduct the flight. All the content is familiar to a twin pilot, but the challenge is, firstly, in flying accurately from the right-hand seat; secondly, in teaching a manoeuvre whilst demonstrating it; and thirdly, in identifying and correcting student errors. Individually, none of these is particularly hard, but putting it all together and delivering an effective and complete lesson is demanding, especially given how much is packed into 3.5 hours in the asymmetric part of the syllabus. Personally, I have found some JAA training over-formalised and narrow at times, but I thought the CRI course was perfect, in that the detailed structure gave you both a precise path to accomplishing the training in a relatively short time and a precise reference for teaching the MEPL rating to your own students.

A few months later I was lucky enough to have a very motivated and capable pilot as my first student. The flight training took 1hr more than the 6hrs minimum, I simply didn't have the experience to teach all the syllabus in the allotted time, and the ground school took a lot more than the 7hrs required. Conducting training to a good standard and being efficient in how the student's time and money is spent is not easy. My respect for professional instructors has increased a lot! I think for an 'occasional' instructor like myself, initial class rating courses are a stretch, because one doesn't have either the ideal level of teaching experience or the ideal level of currency on the training aircraft type. Where I find the CRI most useful is in giving you the ability to instruct in the kind of flying you are already experienced and current on, in my case multi-engine training and conversion to the 421C. This is the motivation, I imagine, behind the JAA's design of these excellent courses. As a twin pilot, I can say that every minute of the MEPL-CRI was worth doing even if I never intended using it.

JAA instrument rating instructor IRI(A)[19] [20]

Holders of a JAA IR with over 200hrs of actual instrument time (or 800hrs IFR flight) can become instructors for the JAA IR and CAA IMC ratings. Like the CRI, the IRI does not need CPL theory or a Class 1 medical. The course is 30-40hrs of ground study and 10hrs flight or FNPT2 training, followed by a skills test. Teaching multi-engine IFR also needs the MEPL-CRI, but the two courses can be combined very efficiently. The IRI is valid three years, and requires a skills test for revalidation.

The leap from zero instructor qualifications to the IRI may seen a considerable one, given the usual career path for instructors is to start as restricted FI(A)s teaching the PPL and perhaps taking years to move to IR training. However, I think the JAA system makes a lot of sense, because an experienced IFR pilot with the right instructor training may be just as well suited to teaching IFR as an experienced FI(A) is with the right IFR training. I don't have a JAA IRI, but based on my FAA experience, I actually found instrument instructing the easiest of the trio of CFI, MEI and CFI-I ratings. VFR stick-and-rudder skills are something of an art, and teaching them is quite different from just applying them. IFR is very algorithmic and codified, and teaching it involves, to a reasonable extent, merely verbalising and explaining the normal processes of IFR flight.

In summary, I think the JAA CRI and IRI are a great combination: relatively inexpensive to train for and an excellent skills developer and refresher. Using the privileges to give occasional recurrent instrument training can be rewarding and cost-effective: two pilots can log the flight time, and, as the instructor, you can learn a lot from the process of teaching and observing your student.

FAA instructor qualifications[21] [22]

The FAA system is a fairly simple one, with three instructor qualifications: the single-engine certified flight instructor (CFI), the multi-engine instructor (MEI) add-on and the instrument instructor (CFI-I) add-on.

The entry requirements are straightforward: you need to have an FAA commercial certificate with instrument rating for the CFI and CFI-I, and a commercial multi-engine class rating for the MEI. There is no ME upgrade to the CFI-I, you just need multi-engine IR privileges in order to teach IFR on twins.

There are three instructor written tests. The Fundamentals of Instructing (FOI) is short and easy. The CFI written test is one of the harder FAA exams. The CFI-I written exam is almost identical to the instrument rating one. These three exams do not require any training endorsement in order for you to sit them, you can study on your own and just take the test.

Each of the three qualifications require an instructor endorsement (but with no minimum training hours specified) and an oral exam and flight check ride from an FAA Designated Pilot Examiner (DPE). The initial instructor qualification (the CFI) usually involves a thorough and demanding session with the DPE, it is always scheduled to start in the morning and can take most of the day. Booking this test also requires a little more planning, because the local FAA office has to be notified and can insist that one of their staff examiners conducts the test. The MEI and CFI-I add-ons are fairly quick and straightforward, especially if you do them with the same DPE as your initial CFI.

I thought the JAA CRI and IRI were worth reviewing in some detail, because they are little-known courses that might be of particular interest to a JAA pilot. For the FAA qualifications, there are many web resources and books available, so I will only mention a few points from my experience that may be useful:

- Getting your initial CFI is quite a lot of work, but the FAA approach is very progressive and flexible. You don't have to complete an approved course at a single school, you can build up to the final check-ride step by step. Get one of the CFI textbooks and study a bit. Do the easy FOI exam. Get a few hours of CFI training and see how you like it, it doesn't need to be with an FAA instructor, you could use a JAA one, and take it from there. If you get hooked, study for the CFI written and plan a couple of weeks in the US;

- If you also have a UK PPL, you could do the CRI (SEPL or MEPL) first; all the JAA training contributes to your FAA CFI, since the principles of teaching and flying from the right hand seat are common to both systems, and there is no requirement for FAA-specific training, beyond getting an instructor to endorse you for the check-ride;

⌒ Remember that you can not get paid for any FAA training in the UK unless you have the parallel JAA CPL and FI qualifications. Paid training on a N-reg airplane requires a DfT waiver. Any training, even unpaid, towards a licence or rating in the UK requires a JAA instructor under the UK ANO. For an FAA instructor to conduct *ab initio* PPL, multi-engine or IR training outside the USA still requires TSA registration and approval. In effect, these regulations limit a "basic" FAA CFI to unpaid recurrent training and BFRs – but, for the PPL/IR, that may be a worthwhile goal.

There is an additional feature of the US system relevant to the experienced multi-engine pilot. You can take your initial CFI certificate on a twin and do the single-engine CFI and CFI-I as add-ons. This may be easier, because the difficult initial test will focus on familiar multi-engine procedures like VMC demos and engine failure drills rather than the various single-engine *ab initio* training manoeuvres.

Hence, for the multi-engine pilot transitioning to the FAA system, the most efficient sequence for getting all the qualifications up to the ATP is

1. Private certificate check ride (following private written);

2. Multi-engine check ride;

3. Combined commercial and multi-engine instrument check ride (following commercial and instrument writtens);

4. Multi-engine initial instructor check ride (following FOI and CFI writtens);

5. Combined single-engine commercial and CFI add-on check ride;

6. CFI-I check ride, may be on a single for both single and twin privileges (following CFI-I written).

Conclusions

Flying regularly plus the JAA IR revalidation or FAA BFR are a fair means of staying safe and current. For many pilots, additional training might be useful, enjoyable and cost-effective. There are a lot of training options available beyond the routine and familiar ones, and, with some careful planning, you can achieve multiple training goals from a single course.

Electing to do additional FNPT2 simulator training is probably the most effective way for a PPL/IR to maintain skills and currency at a higher level. US type-specific simulator schools are a good resource for pilots of the more complex GA aircraft.

For the JAA License holder, the CRI and IRI courses offer an accessible step-up qualification which is also a good source of recurrent training and skills improvement.

For the FAA private instrument pilot, the equivalent is probably the upgrade to the commercial certificate. Under both systems, the more daunting advanced qualifications can, to some extent, be broken down into manageable steps.

This rather long article is still only a brief overview of the many topics covered. The *PPL/IR Europe* website forum (www.pplir.org/pplir/) is a good place to draw on the experience of members who are expert in one or more of these subjects.

References and notes

(1) JAA IR renewal, see LASORS Section E1.5
www.caa.co.uk (search for LASORS under publications to get latest edition)

(2) FAA IR currency, see 14 CFR 61.57
www.access.gpo.gov/nara/cfr/waisidx_06/14cfr61_06.html

(3) PPL/IR list of UK IREs/CREs
www.pplir.org/index.php?option=com_content&task=view&id=201
(restricted access to **PPL/IR Europe** members only)

(4) Examples of modern FTD types
www.flyelite.ch/en/index.php

(5) Example of FAA scenario-based training syllabus for the PPL/IR
www.faa.gov/education_research/training/fits/training/aircraft/media/MTSU.pdf

(6) JAA TGL10 PRNAV crew training requirements
www.ecacnav.com/downloads/Tgl10jaa.pdf (see section 10.5)

(7) Example of FAA scenario-based training syllabus for the Garmin
GNS530/430
www.faa.gov/education_research/training/fits/training/aircraft/media/
GNS530_430_Syllabus.pdf

(8) Jeppesen 'Instrument Procedures Guide'
www.jeppesen.com
Home >Products & Services >Aviation Training >Pilot Training >Jeppesen
Aviation Information Materials >Jeppesen Instrument Procedures Guide

(9) 'Instrument Flight Procedures' by Jens Gjerlev
www.aurinko.no/fcts.htm

(10) I have been loose with my terminology in this article because the term
'simulator' formally refers to an approved full-motion trainer, typically for
turbine aircraft. The GA "simulators" are flight and procedure training
devices, with a variety of FAA and JAA designations.

(11) US simulator training schools:
  ⌒ **Simcom** (www.simulator.com): wide range of GA aircraft courses
    and generic ME and SE IFR refreshers
  ⌒ **RTC** (www.rtcpilot.com): wide range of GA aircraft courses and
    generic ME and SE IFR refreshers

⌒ **Flight Safety International** (www.flightsafety.com): courses on high-performance Cessna, Piper and Beech types

⌒ **CAE Simuflite** (www.caesimuflite.com): focused on turboprops and business jets

(12) FAA commercial written test software (highly recommended)
www.dauntless-soft.com/PRODUCTS/GroundSchool/commercial.asp
(Study the books and practice with this software until you can score over 90%.
The better your written test score, the easier time you will have in the Oral exam.)

(13) FAA commercial requirements, see 14 CFR 61.129 also 121-133
www.access.gpo.gov/nara/cfr/waisidx_06/14cfr61_06.html

(14) JAA CPL requirements, see LASORS Section D1 (see 1 above)

(15) Schools providing JAA CPL Theory courses:
⌒ **Atlantic Flight Training** (www.flyaft.com)
⌒ **Ground Training Services** (www.gtserv.co.uk)
⌒ **Cranfield Aviation Training School** (www.cranfieldaviation.co.uk)

(16) Excellent website for free samples of JAA Theory paper content (www.atpl.gs)

(17) JAA class rating instructor (SPA), see LASORS Section H3, (see 1 above)

(18) JAA CRI course examples:
⌒ **Bournemouth Commercial Flight Training Centre** (www.bcft.org.uk)
⌒ **On Track Aviation** (www.ontrackaviation.com)

(19) JAA instrument rating instructor (IRI(A)), see LASORS Section H2, (see 1 above)

(20) JAA IRI course examples
⌒ **Bournemouth Commercial Flight Training Centre** (www.bcft.org.uk)
⌒ **On Track Aviation** (www.ontrackaviation.com)

(21) FAA instructor qualifications, see 14 CFR 61.181-189
www.access.gpo.gov/nara/cfr/waisidx_06/14cfr61_06.html

(22) Example of FAA instructor courses:
⌒ **CFI** (www.flyoft.com/cfi.php)
⌒ **MEI** (www.flyoft.com/mei.php)
⌒ **CFII** (www.flyoft.com/cf2.php)

Piper PA-30, Twin Comanche shared by *PPL/IR Europe* members Alan South and Julian Scarfe. Photo © Philip Whiteman

Twin Commander turboprop, formerly owned by *PPL/IR Europe* member Ole Henriksen

Cessna 421C owned by **PPL/IR Europe** member Vasa Babic

Cessna 421C panel

SR22 Cirrus owned by **PPL/IR Europe** member Anthony Bowles

G-HEJB's panel

PA46 Malibu, formerly owned by PPL/IR Europe member David Findon

Panel from a different PA46 Malibu, part owned by **PPL/IR Europe** Steve Copeland

DA42 Twinstar G-DJET owned by *PPL/IR Europe* Peter Bondar

Left and right-hand views of G-DJET 's panel

Socata TB20 Trinidad owned by **PPL/IR Europe** member Peter Holy

N113AC's panel

Socata TB10 Tobago flown by **PPL/IR Europe** member Andy Reohorn

PPL/IR Europe member Steve Copeland flying a Cessna 172 setting the pace with a Cessna 182 en route to Quiberon in France

Mooney M20J owned by **PPL/IR Europe** member David Sowray. Photo by Sally Turner

Siai Marchetti SF260 owned by **PPL/IR Europe** member Marco Gavazzi. Photo by Sally Turner

SECTION 2

Aircraft selection

Section Contents

1 Aircraft choice

By Timothy Nathan

The instrument pilot has a wide range of aircraft to choose from. IFR and even airways flight can be achieved in any airframe from the Cessna 152 upwards. This article attempts to lay out some of the factors that will help the IFR pilot select the right aircraft for the mission profile. The discussion is limited to fixed wing GA. If rotary is your thing, you probably already know more about helicopters than me.

The basic choices for the average GA IFR pilot come down to the following:

- Buy, share or rent?

- New, recent or old?

- Single or twin?

- De-icing?

- Piston, turboprop or jet?

⌒ Avgas or Jet A1?

⌒ Glass or six-pack?

⌒ Autopilot? FD?

⌒ Weather avoidance?

⌒ Traffic avoidance?

⌒ Pressurised, installed or portable oxygen or nothing?

These choices are far from independent from each other, and, especially if you are renting, several of them may be taken for you, but, for a price, most combinations are available, so we will consider them each in turn.

But before we do, it is vital to consider in detail what you want the aircraft for.

Mission profile

You must be interested in IFR flight in Europe. If you weren't, you wouldn't be reading this book. But what kinds of flight do you normally make? Do you need to get from Northern England to Southern Spain every weekend without fail with little time to spare, or do you mainly potter 100nm for a decent meal on a Sunday if the weather is good? Do you just need to get yourself and your laptop to business meetings, or do your spouse, nanny and five kids pack seven big suitcases for a weekend away? How many aircraft do you fly? Does one aircraft have to meet your VFR bimbling, aerobatic and long range touring needs, or do you have a workhorse and a plaything? Will you always have 800m of tarmac, or do you want the flexibility to fly into short strips?

Range, payload and speed are the big calculation in all touring aircraft, and each tends to oppose the other. To get all three starts to get expensive. But if you can compromise on one, the other two become achievable. For example, Mooneys and Bonanzas can go fast a reasonably long way, and the DA42 and some Robins can go slowly a seriously long way, but only if you limit the payload to two people. If you want to pack more people in and are happy to go somewhat slower then the Cherokee 6/Lance family might work for you and so on.

But if you don't sit down and work out what you want to do, you will never be able to pick the right aircraft. So don't be seduced by the avionics, the paint job or the leather; pick up the POH and work out if the aircraft will do what you want.

Buy, share or rent?

All three options have obvious benefits, so we won't spend any time on them – if you rent, you can walk away from the cracked crankcase; if you share the costs become manageable; if you own outright, the aircraft is always there when you want it, in the state you left it – but it might be worth dwelling on some of the less obvious pitfalls. I take no particular position, but have done all three and might be able to help you avoid some issues.

If you rent or share, there are usually some recency requirements which can be irksome and sometimes prevent you making the flight you need. You might see that as a disadvantage, but equally, bear in mind that no-one is looking over the shoulder of the sole owner. He or she is free to blast off at any time. How much can you rely on yourself to stay current and not get into bad habits?

If you are in a group, there will be others to talk things over with. They might spot something in the POH you had missed, you might get together and write SOPs. On the other hand one of the others might do a hard landing without telling anyone, leaving you with a nosewheel failure on next flight, then no aircraft for nine months. It happens. All the time.

Another potential disadvantage of rental or groups is that equipment might not be maintained, replaced or even fitted because the majority of users don't see the need. For example, if you are the only one who wants to fly in a particular piece of airspace where PRNAV or high frequency is mandated, you may find that you are simply prohibited from that airspace.

My advice is that anyone joining a group, or forming one, has a clearly written condition that the aircraft is to be maintained as a full IFR aircraft capable of flight in all European airspace. My second related advice would be to have a small group and conditions which give a higher priority to people making long trips (which they should invite the other members on where practicable). It isn't uncommon for groups to have a member who books a one hour flight on virtually every Saturday afternoon of the year.

And remember that while some groups run in perfect equanimity for many years, it is not uncommon for them to collapse in acrimony and financial loss. Be sure that your co-owners think like you, share your ethics and want to do the same kind of flying. Otherwise it will all end in tears.

And a word for the sole owner. In my opinion, you must always be in a financial position to replace the engine(s) tomorrow, or to accept a total loss of the aircraft without ruining yourself. Aeroplanes are a consumable, not an investment.

New, recent or old?
Are you going to pre-order a VLJ or DA-42, buy a two year old Columbia or look for a thirty year old venerable old bus? Economists and accountants will be able to justify any of these options, and we each reach our own conclusions.

The arguments for new will include:

⌒ You can order exactly what you want rather than take whatever is on the market;

⌒ The factory warranty;

⌒ It will have the latest gadgets such as glass.

For a recent used model:

⌒ The manufacturing bugs will have been ironed out;

⌒ The initial depreciation has already been lost;

⌒ The equipment will be recent and probably still works;

For old aircraft:

⌒ Cheap to buy;

⌒ History of experience of model characteristics/established SOPs;

⌒ Zero depreciation.

However, each of the positives above can be seen as negative for the alternatives. For example, consider the DA-42 which crashed because the pilot did not know to charge the batteries properly before departure. That happened because of a lack of established lore. It won't happen again, because all DA-42 pilots will have that experience rammed down their throats. On the other hand, owning an old aircraft can be an ongoing project management experience as you try and find spares while you make do and mend, and you struggle to ensure that it complies with the most recent regulatory requirements (it is not uncommon for an avionics refit to cost more than the value of the aircraft).

Single or twin?

This is the biggest decision, and the one I will spend longest on. It is no co-incidence that the proportion of twins amongst IFR pilots is much higher than in the VFR world. It is not just that IFR pilots have nothing better to do with their money, it is because many consider that the utility and safety of a twin tends to be higher.

There are many people who fly extensively in IFR in singles, and with great success; there are those who try and find safety arguments to justify their decision. In my opinion the principle case for operating a piston single is economic. If you can afford to fly a single, but not a twin, that is an excellent reason for operating a single.

However, if you can afford a turbine single, whether turboprop or pure jet, the calculation changes again. These engines are so reliable, and drive so many redundant systems, that an average SET is probably both safer and more capable than an average MEP.

The comparison that follows is between the average SEP and MEP, let's say a Seneca and a TB10, which is likely to be the choice in hand for most readers of this book for the foreseeable future.

Icing

The commonest reason that people seem to cancel flights in non de-iced aircraft is icing. If icing is going to be present from the MSA up to FL100 you really cannot even think of getting the non-de-iced aircraft out of the hangar.

There are de-iced singles – de-icing is available on PA46, BE36, some Mooneys and C210 - but they are relatively few and far between and the weight penalty can become quite burdensome. De-icing on an MEP is the rule rather than the exception.

A major protection in a non-de-iced aircraft is to have a large gap between cruising speed and stalling speed. A Mooney cruises at 100 Kts above its stall speed, a basic C172 45 Kts. That ratio can make a big difference when you are carrying a lot of ice.

Finally, remember that de-icing is not an all or nothing option. If you cannot carry full airframe de-icing because of weight or cost, you should still think about prop and windscreen de-icing to help you escape an unexpected ice encounter.

Speed
Although at first glance going fast seems to be a luxury rather than a necessity, it becomes very relevant indeed when faced with a strong headwind. 50kt winds are not unusual at higher levels. This means that a 160kt aircraft will be making good 110 Kts, whereas at 120kt the ground speed is 70 Kts, a disproportionate difference.

There are fast SEPs, but on average MEPs tend to be faster. Of course, this is as much as argument for a Bonanza over an Arrow as it is for an MEP over an SEP.

Efficiency
However, let us not forget the inefficiencies of dragging that second engine around. Even an Arrow is using less than half the fuel of an Aztec to go at 80% of the speed, and the comparison is even less favourable with a modern VLA. This is not only a financial saving but an environmental one as well.

Payload
This is where twins, and particularly Aztecs and the larger Cessna twins, really score. Typically these aircraft can fly the length and breadth of Europe with four, six or even more people on board. Even the capable singles cannot match this. They become fuel limited very quickly with four people and their golf clubs.

Crosswind
Fewer and fewer airfields are offering a cross runway. A typical SEP crosswind capability of 15 Kts means that the number of days which are outside limits at one end of the flight or the other reach significant levels. The demonstrated capability of mid range MEPs is typically 25 Kts, but I know from personal experience that most can cope with 40 Kts with no difficulty. SEPs can also be "pushed" but, especially the faster ones, are practically limited to around 20 Kts. This can present a real impediment to reliable despatch.

Runway requirements
This is where most MEPs lose out, though probably not to the extent that you might think. The Aztec will operate at MTOW in and out of 470m hard runway, or about

700m of short, hard grass. If you are going to operate an MEP safely you need the full accelerate-stop balanced field length, typically 700m or more. This does mean that many strips are out of bounds to many MEPs, which is a definite limitation. So if you need an IFR tourer that can operate out of strips, you might need to think about the C172/182 series.

Engine failure

I have had nine engine failures in my flying career. I know that they happen. This is why I always want a plan B available to cover the eventuality. Plan B in a twin is to divert at leisure. Plan B in a single should be to make a forced landing in a field. But that's rather difficult in hill fog, or even a 200ft cloud base, or at night, or over water, or over mountains. So if you fly a single and want to ensure that there is a plan B you are limited to flying over farmland, during the day, when the weather is reasonably good. This limits mission capability to such an extent that you might ask "why bother with an instrument qualification?"

Most SEP pilots will not plan to take-off or land when the cloud base is below 200ft above DA. That means a minimum of 450ft, sometimes higher. They will also often limit themselves to a visibility where a forced landing has at least some hope of success, maybe 1500m. To limit your flying to days when the weather betters these minima is to place quite a restriction above the limits you have learnt to fly to in your IR training (though closely match the limitations and recommendations on a UK IMC rating.)

Most GA twins are not certified to be able to continue flying in the event of an engine failure below 200ft. Twin training concentrates on failures above 200ft, recovery from such a failure and continuation of the flight. Unfortunately not enough emphasis is placed on the fact that below 200ft the most prudent action is normally to shut down both engines and make a forced landing. The argument continues that if either engine fails, the result is a forced landing, and therefore the risk is at least doubled (I say "at least" because engines are marginally more likely to fail on a twin because of greater vibration and longer control runs.)

This increased risk is real and must be taken into account by the twin owner, but is offset by having the second engine available in the cruise, especially when conditions dictate that a forced landing is unlikely to be successful (water, mountains, night, low cloud etc).

Furthermore the time for which the aircraft is exposed to EFATO risk is very small (less than 15 seconds per flight) compared to the time spent exposed to risk in a single. Also, the pilot can do a great deal to mitigate the risk (using the full runway, rotating at blue line, avoiding built up areas in the take-off path etc). Of course, the SEP pilot can also mitigate risk by flying high, thus bringing more runways into gliding range, and this, in itself, is an argument for flying IFR in a single.

Less protection in a forced landing in a twin

In the event of a forced landing, uninjured survival of the passengers is said to be less likely in an MEP because the aircraft is going faster and the momentum is greater, the occupants are not protected by the engine going ahead of them and that the gear may be up and therefore not in a position to absorb impact.

This consideration is mitigated by the fact that a forced landing is less likely.

Electrical or other systems failure

In a single, almost as serious as an engine failure is an alternator failure in or above IMC. With no way of navigating or communicating you are left with some pretty unpleasant choices...flying triangles in the hope that someone will notice, then unrehearsed formation flying in cloud, or maybe dead reckoning to where you hope the sea is and then hoping that your guess at QNH is reasonably accurate.

Similarly, loss of your single vacuum pump can be pretty fatal, particularly if you identify the symptoms late. There are, of course, a small number of singles with redundant ancillaries, particularly alternators and suction pumps, and that is what makes those aircraft more suited to transport flying than 172s and PA28s, but you have to hunt for them.

Initial and recurrent training

There is an overhead to gaining a twin rating, and particularly to gain and maintain an IR on a twin. Renting a twin to do that training can be very expensive, especially as there is more to do than on a single. Another strong economic factor in favour of the single.

Currency

Most people agree that the requirements for currency are greater in a twin than a single, both because the immediate actions following an engine failure are urgent and need to be off pat, and because the systems are more complex, so need greater knowledge and understanding.

In an MEP two flights of a hour each per month, with a practice EFATO every four months, would seem to be a sensible minimum, and if you cannot do that, it may not be wise to operate an MEP.

However, SEP pilots, particularly those with IRs, also need to remain current. The vital actions after an engine failure – converting speed to height, seeking a field, setting up a pattern, mayday call, briefing passengers, security, shutdown and so on – are scarcely less onerous than those required in a twin, and should be practiced regularly.

Fuel systems

Some MEPs have stupidly complex fuel systems, which have historically brought down aircraft which departed with enough fuel on board. This is a consideration when looking at twins. Talk to owners and read the POH. Will you be able to cope with the fuel system when you are already dealing with another system failure in turbulent cloud?

Greater risks taken by twin pilots

There is an argument, called risk compensation, that no matter how safe a piece of equipment or transport is made, overall safety is not affected because the user will take greater risks until the risk level reaches the same point as it had been on the less safe equipment.

Thus, a twin is not safer than a single, because the pilot will choose to fly over water, in icing, at night, to IFR minima, where the prudent single pilot would not.

But the twin pilot taking the same risk as an SEP pilot is able to operate in more difficult environments at the same risk. Which means that the mission is flown in an MEP where it might well have been abandoned in an SEP.

Market factors

With the notable exception of the DA-42, everything exciting that is happening in the GA market is happening to singles – Cirrus, Columbia, PA46, VLAs, VLJs, SETs are examples. If you want an MEP it will either be old or, at best, a recent example of an old design (Seneca and Baron for example.) If you want composite and glass and all the other good stuff that goes with the purchase of a new or recent aircraft you are limited to either a single or the rather gutless DA-42 (which does not have many of the advantages of classic MEPs, such as payload and performance.)

Resale values of MEPs are at an all time low, which reflects both on their desirability (driven by fuel price and JAA mismanagement of licensing and ratings) and price. If you want an MEP, now is a great time to buy one, but be prepared to write-off the purchase price. Any money spent on it will probably be lost.

Eurocontrol

Possibly a small point in the overall costs of running a twin, but do remember that nearly all twins are heavy enough to incur Eurocontrol charges for IFR flights, whereas even the heaviest and best performance SEPs are light enough to avoid them. These charges can add more than €60 per hour onto the costs of an IFR flight. Remember also that all night flying is IFR, so even an evening VMC bimble in the twin can get expensive.

Cost and engineering

The cost of operating an MEP is not just a question of feeding fuel to the second engine, but having engineers spend double their time on the engines, props and ancillaries plus all the extra time and parts consumed by wobbly wheels and props, de-icing, separate heater and so on. An annual on an MEP can easily result in an €14,000 invoice, even if nothing major is found. By the time you have sent the heater off for an overhaul, replaced the hoses and had the de-icing boots patched up, the money spent on the routine part of the maintenance becomes chicken-feed.

It makes far more economic sense to operate a single.

But the "having more to go wrong" argument cuts both ways. Yes, it is expensive, but it also means that you have redundant systems to ensure that you can continue your flight. Losing an alternator or fuel pump is a non-event. You can even take-off and return to base because you are carrying redundancy.

But the main reason that I personally am willing to pay more to operate a twin is that I simply don't enjoy flying over inhospitable environments, or in inhospitable conditions, if I am constantly worrying about the effect of an engine, alternator or vacuum pump failure. I know they fail, and my constant worrying about what I am going to do when they do fail just takes all the joy away for me. Many people don't suffer from these anxieties, typically saying "the engine doesn't know it is over water."

But so long as I have a mission profile which means long trips over water, ice and mountains, at night and in bad weather, it will always be a twin for me. But equally there are many **PPL/IR Europe** members who have put thousands of hours on SEPs in IFR without any serious incident, so you may consider my position to be too doom laden…your call.

Piston, turboprop or jet? Avgas or Jet A1?

Many readers of this book will not be in a position to consider either a single or twin turboprop or jet, and the choice will simply be a one of how many piston engines and whether they should be avgas or diesel.

However, there is today such a range of high-end options for the private buyer that we should not ignore them.

The VLJ – typically a four-seater light single with a fan jet in the back – is a very tempting proposition for the serious tourer. There is very little ownership history yet, so we don't know what the problems will be, but the authorities, airlines and professional pilots alike are very concerned about the capability of any single pilot, let alone one without professional training and the backup of an ops department, SOPs and a chief pilot, to operate at airliner speeds and at airliner levels. Of course the onboard systems, such as glass cockpits and automated engine and fuel management systems appear to make the pilot's life easier, but equally there are a lot of buttons being pressed without the critical eye of a monitoring second pilot. I know, as a latter-day executive jet pilot, that things can go very wrong very quickly. Will a single PPL be able to handle these things at over 400 Kts? I don't know, but I share the concerns.

The SET is a more established alternative and, for those that can afford them, another very tempting option. Once the capital has been laid out, and until the engine requires major work, they offer a reasonably economical way to relatively high performance and capability.

The METs, such as the King Air series, seem to be a relatively unpopular amongst private owners. This is probably because their performance is only a little superior to the high end MEPs, but the costs, particularly the engine replacement costs, can be a lot higher and indeed somewhat frightening unless you are seriously rich. If you can get a "power by the hour" maintenance option the risks are mitigated, but remain enough to deter all but the wealthy.

The big advantage of all the above is one of fuel availability. It is becoming harder and harder to find avgas at larger and regional airfields, and supplies sometimes dry up entirely for whole regions for substantial periods of time (this happens repeatedly in Italy and has afflicted France as well in recent years.) On the other hand, Jet A1 is available everywhere, even very small airfields, because of the range and class of aircraft that use it, from small helicopters to A380s.

Jet has also traditionally been much cheaper than avgas. But this situation is about to change for the pleasure pilot, with significant extra levies being raised on the private use of jet fuel. The enforcement of the levies would at first glance seem to be problematical, only time will tell, but one way and another, now does not seem the time to go jet for the sake of fuel cost savings.

If you cannot afford a turbine and you still want the advantages of being able to use jet fuel, there remains the option of the diesel pistons. You can buy one of the small range of aircraft that are being manufactured with diesel engines (these are all SEPs except the DA-42) or you can have an avgas aircraft converted to diesel. There remain some disadvantages. Initial cost is high; the engines weigh more, so eat into the payload (though this is somewhat offset by lower fuel consumption) and there are big question marks about the reliability of these engines. However, the reliability is bound to improve as the manufacturers and engineers gain experience and data, and cost and weight are also likely to fall as uptake increases. It is a shame that the biggest spur to the adoption of diesel, the big tax break on fuel, is disappearing for the private owner.

Glass or six-pack?

These days it is very rare to peek into the flight deck of a CAT or Bizjet and see anything less than a full glass panel, AoA orientated FD and auto-throttles. Such equipment is seen as de rigueur for a two-crew IFR-only operation above the weather in a fully controlled environment. However, look at the panel of the average aircraft flown autonomously by a single-crew in filthy weather close to the ground and the chances are you will see a six-pack of mechanical, raw data dials.

However, GA is finally beginning to catch up with the higher end of the market in the availability of glass instrumentation. The first step – GPS based, data rich, moving map navigation systems such as the GNS430/530 – are now to be seen in most IFR equipped aircraft. Indeed, since the implementation of BRNAV requirements it has been difficult to operate without them. There is no doubt that the GPS moving map, with airspace, tracks and procedures superimposed, is the biggest step forward in improving IFR situational awareness since the HSI.

But the next generation of fully glass cockpit, whereby all flight data is presented on two computer display screens, the horizon is 26cm wide and back-lit rather than 10cm and ambient-lit (and thus much more likely to be noticed in peripheral vision) and the scan is reduced to two large, information packed instruments is a quantum leap beyond even the moving map GPS display. It is the first real step forward since instrument flight was invented in the 1920s. Anyone who has used glass will tell you that it improves their flying, both in terms of comfort and safety, while reducing pilot stress and fatigue.

Why would anyone fly with anything less? Although cost is something of a factor, there is no doubt that in the long run it must be cheaper to produce electronics than mechanical instrumentation. The answer lies mainly in the huge number of aging and aged aircraft that make up the bulk of the GA fleet. Although it is theoretically possible to convert many of these aircraft to glass, the economics make no sense. Yet it also does not make sense to throw them away for lack of glass.

So, how important is it to you to fly glass? If you have learnt your instrument skills on glass you may find it a struggle to convert onto the six-pack. But even if you have good six-pack skills, you are more likely to arrive unstressed and equanimous with glass. But you may decide that part of the challenge is taken away, that you want to stretch yourself by using raw data. You may think that if all the difficult bits are taken away, you may as well go by commercial transport.

There is also the small aside, of particular resonance to me as I love to fly in the Arctic, that many glass installations are not cleared for use North of 70N. That may or may not be a consideration for you, but recently prevented a friend with a DA-42 from joining me on an Arctic trip. (See pages 152-153 for some photographs of a recent trip to the North Pole).

It all comes down to mission. The choice is yours.

Autopilot? Fight director?

There are those who seem to think that using an autopilot detracts from the experience of self-flown IFR transport. After all, when does self-flown not mean self-flown? There are even those who say that to use an autopilot is to allow your skills to dwindle, some even seem to think that it is not macho to use one.

This is baloney. Pilot workload is a factor in many, if not most, IFR accidents, and most IFR accidents are in multi crew aircraft. For the single pilot to think that he can plan, replan, brief and execute an IFR flight safely while keeping the aircraft within tight flight parameters while in turbulent IMC is just too ambitious.

A serious IFR aircraft should have a reliable, functioning autopilot. In my opinion, it is enough that that autopilot can hold heading and altitude – pilots should be sufficiently aware of their flight parameters to fly heading rather than course – but it is also helpful to have ROC/ROD and VOR/LOC/GS couplings. Altitude capture can help eliminate the real risk of altitude busts, and PRNAV is likely to mean that coupling to an auto-slew HSI becomes mandatory in some airspace. There are dangers inherent in ROC control, as the autopilot can quite blithely drive the aircraft into a deep stall as it continues to try and climb despite engine power loss or icing.

A flight director is usually an add-on to the autopilot and makes hand flying much easier and more accurate, as it tells you where to put the aircraft on the AI. In my opinion it comes under the heading of "nice to have" rather than essential, but all else being equal it certainly adds to the value of an IFR aircraft.

Weather avoidance?

The amount of serious weather that you are likely to have to avoid over Europe is rather small. Thunderstorms are a relatively rare phenomenon and the chances of entering one are overall rather slim. However, if you have no way of avoiding them, you have to think about cancelling every flight on a day when they are forecast, and that is going to interfere with your flying program out of all proportion with the actual chances of entering a cell. So if you need a despatch reliability you are going to need either stormscope or radar. The choice between them is a matter of cost, weight and reliability and is dealt with elsewhere (see Vasa Babic's chapter on Self Flown GA IFR transport in Europe, p108). The only thing I would add is that weather information is much better presented as an overlay on glass than on a separate screen.

Traffic avoidance?

There are a growing number of technologies to portray the presence of other squawking aircraft. Like weather, these can be on a separate screen or on glass. My personal view about TCAS is very sceptical. Firstly, the most recent and tragic mid-air was to a greater or lesser extent *caused* by TCAS rather than prevented. Secondly, there have been no recorded mid-air collisions involving civilian aircraft in uncontrolled IMC ever in Europe. Therefore, in my opinion, the best that TCAS can do is to give you comfort, and that comfort is unwarranted. If you want to spend money on that comfort, be my guest, but there may be better ways you can improve safety with that money.

Pressurised, oxygen or neither?

One of the great benefits of IFR flying, ironically, is the ability to climb out of weather to the clear and calm air above.

Quite often it is possible to take off in filthy drizzle and to pop out of the tops at 5,000 feet. Under these circumstances there is no need for oxygen, but often the tops, particularly of unstable, turbulent and ice-bearing clouds can be significantly higher. But, with the exception of thunderstorms, it is unusual for the tops of weather to be above 15,000 feet, and therefore many people think of around 18,000 feet as a sweet place to be for touring. Depending on the engine and how it is aspirated this altitude can provide improved TAS and range as well.

Opinions, and regulation, vary as to how high, and for how long, it is safe to fly without oxygen. Oxygen starvation is insidious, and the pilot will usually not recognise it in himself, and he may be incapacitated or dead without ever realising anything is amiss. There is evidence that tolerance of reduced oxygen availability is lower at night, and it is certainly worse for smokers and the unfit. Personally, I will fly at FL100 for any length of time, whether by day or night, and will fly at FL130 for about an hour or less. Others must determine their own tolerance, possibly by using one of the devices available to measure blood oxygen saturation.

If you plan to fly above these levels you must use oxygen. The choices come down to a portable kit, of which there is a great variety at a range of costs (both in terms of money and weight), a plumbed-in system or pressurisation.

If you fly above about 18,000 feet you will need masks rather than cannulae. Masks are generally uncomfortable, and flying in the 20-25,000 feet band, even with masks can result in loss of concentration, headaches and fatigue – not a great way to enter a precision approach and then a business meeting or fun day out. If that is your height band, you might start thinking about pressurisation.

Pressurisation is needed if you are going to fly regularly above about 24,000 feet, or ever up to 30,000 feet. It is costly to buy, can be costly to maintain, can impose life limitations on the airframe and anyway needs to be supplemented by an oxygen system in case of failure. However, it has the considerable advantage that your passengers can remain blissfully unaware and undisturbed by oxygen equipment, and is not time limited.

Plumbed-in oxygen systems seem to me to have few advantages over portable ones. Above all, you cannot choose to remove the system from the aircraft for weight and space reasons, but also they are subject to certification requirements, must be refilled from an expensive aviation source and are usually heavier than portable systems.

Portable systems come in a variety of guises; it is important to get a system that can be filled at a dive shop at a fraction of the air-side price, and it is worth investing in a light, high capacity system, preferably with metered flow to cannulae.

Summary

I have tried to go through most of the important choices you will need to make when choosing the aircraft that you are going to trust your life to. There is no "best aircraft." We all take our own decisions according to our mission, our means, our preferences and our prejudices. Just because I am very happy with my Aztec and someone else loves their TB10, C421 or Citation is no reason at all to make you think that you need the same thing. It is a totally personal choice that you must make in an informed and careful way.

It all depends on how important it is to achieve the flight, and the timescales. If it is a business imperative to arrive at the planned destination on time and unruffled, you are going to need a well equipped MEP (or turbine) with oxygen, de-icing and weather avoidance.

If you use your aircraft for leisure and are content to have a substantial proportion of your flights cancelled because of weather, then an SEP with basic equipment may be all you need.

You pays your money and you takes your choice.

I would like to thank Vasa Babic and Kevin Horne for their considerable assistance in preparing this chapter.

2　IFR on a budget

By Nigel Everett

Sir Thomas Lipton, the grocer, once answered a questioner:

> *If you need to ask how much it costs to own*
> *a J Class yacht, you can't afford it.*

The same may perhaps be one view of private IFR flying but amongst the members of **PPL/IR Europe** there may be one or two more like myself for whom cost is an important consideration but not sufficient to rule out IFR flying altogether. While learned and even lively debates can be held as to the relative safety and convenience of, say, a piston twin as compared with a turboprop single, there are some out there who just fly what they reasonably can afford and settle for what convenience that may offer while limiting the scope of their IFR flying in a less than perfect machine so as to leave a reasonable margin of safety. If you have engaged in discussion with your spouse about the relative merits of, say, agreeing to pay your share of the cost of an IFR approved GPS set as opposed to, say, upgrading the kitchen, then you are probably down with me amongst the lower orders of the private IFR world.

Contrary to the generally held belief, the holder of an IR is not a pilot of exceptional natural flying ability – merely a pilot with an exceptionally deep pocket and a high degree of determination. Over 90% of those who pass the theoretical knowledge test eventually go on to pass the skill test as well, although some may have to make quite a few attempts before they succeed. The pocket must be deep enough to find something like ten thousand pounds to get the rating and the candidate will also have to go through the tedium of memorising volumes of information, much of which may seem supremely irrelevant to private IFR operation. If life is for living, is this a sensible way to spend a large part of it, or might the same time, money and effort be more fruitfully spent on some less anal activity?

In my own case, my work frequently took me to all sorts of destinations around the South of Britain and I discovered that flying was often a far more satisfying way to travel than pounding the motorways and sometimes – not often – it was genuinely quicker on a door to door basis. One of the greatest delights for the VFR business pilot is to sail blithely over gridlock on the M25 en-route to a destination on the other side of London. However, when you get there it is best not to mention your means of transport as this will encourage suspicions that you are very rich and, if selling, overcharging or, if buying, able to pay well over the odds. It's a tricky situation that is not solved either by simply turning up in a taxi or on your folding bike and saying nothing about your journey. They are likely to assume that you are an alcoholic who has lost his driving licence.

I found with the passing of time that the frequency with which VFR flights were weathered off, about 50% in summer and 75% in winter, propelled me towards getting an IR and the discovery that the costs of getting it could be classed in my case as business expenses, and therefore tax and VAT free, were what clinched it. Looking back, I am bound to say that I enjoyed the challenge, although there were various set backs and times when I wondered whether to throw in the towel. I think that I emerged from it all a far more competent, professional and safe pilot than I had been and the IR has, for me, turned flying into a practical form of transport which, especially when crossing water, can be more convenient and sometimes cheaper than any alternative.

The yawning gap

When I did my flight tests I was examined solely on VOR, DME, ILS and NDB (such larks we had!) and at revalidation time these continue to be "the knowledge", so far as the examiner is concerned, although I am now supposed to demonstrate competence with any other equipment fitted, which in my case will be a very basic autopilot and a Garmin GNS430 (the kitchen upgrade got put off). I have a yen to demonstrate my aptitude with our aeroplane's cigar lighter during the test, but I suppose that this is not a good time to exhibit frivolity of any sort. If the examiner was serious about my proficiency with the other kit he/she would invite me to fly an ILS on my unslaved autopilot down to minimum and as for the Garmin 430, I could be examined all day and still have covered only a small part of its capability. However, I have never, in fact, been invited to show anything much more than an ability to get the moving map up and I yearn to be asked how to find my TAS, the current wind, the nearest airfield with a runway over 1,000 metres and its frequencies, how to insert an extra waypoint in a flight plan, how to change the map from North Up to Track Up and how to paint a specific course line to a destination, I rather suspect that some examiners, living their entire professional lives within the narrow constraints of their own hallowed system, would not know the answers to these things, in any case. So renewal day calls for a little revision on some arcane skills, such as to how fly holds and NDB approaches without first setting up either the procedure or at least the Final Approach Track on the moving map. This serves as an annual reminder of the yawning gap between actual IFR flying and passing the skill test and it also reminds you that the range of equipment desirable for real IFR in all conditions exceeds greatly the limited facilities of an IFR training aeroplane.

Of course, you can fly IFR adequately with no more than the minimum equipment required for an aeroplane to be legal on airways and if you can afford no more than that, then you will have to contrive to manage with what little you have. The important thing is to recognise the limitations that this will impose in convenience and safety and to plan your flying accordingly. What I propose to consider here are what additions you could make to the basic kit, if you could afford them, and how these may improve your convenience and safety. The corollary to such comments is that without the extra convenience or safety offered you must learn to tailor your plans accordingly. Yer pays yer money and yer takes yer choice.

Autopilot

Overload is the enemy of accurate and safe IFR flying and an autopilot, be it no more than a humble wing leveller, can greatly reduce the workload at crucial sectors of the flight. Those who have never flown with one imagine that they come into their own on long stretches of straight and level but their real virtue is that you can secure your heading, say, on an intermediate leg of an approach and then allow your mind, now freed up from constant attention to maintaining a heading, to consider thoroughly the next parts of the procedure and generally to get ahead of the game. The difference between an IFR approach flown while you struggle to keep up with the never ending demands on your attention and the approach where you are truly on top of everything is the difference between a pilot who is a danger and one who is competent and feels fulfilled. An autopilot, intelligently used, can create that difference.

Power

Power means speed, which can reduce a journey that would otherwise call for two legs to just one, which saves time and money. Shorter journey times are likely to make for a fresher pilot, which makes for safety. More importantly, however, power means a greater rate of climb and in Northern Europe this will mean a greater ability to punch through the zone of maximum airframe icing, usually two or three thousand feet thick, before much ice has built up. It will also mean a higher ceiling, giving a greater chance of getting above the weather, always provided that you also have oxygen. Without power and oxygen you may have to remain below the freezing level and this may exclude you from the airways or even take you below Minimum Safety Altitude, in which case you should not be flying IFR. Lack of power makes winter IFR a significantly less practical possibility.

Oxygen

In IFR flying terms a portable oxygen system for one or two people is not that expensive - perhaps less than a thousand pounds - and you may be able to pick up second hand equipment as it is in common use in the gliding world. If you fly a powerful aeroplane, especially if turbocharged, and thus able to maintain full power into the higher flight levels, you would be wasting a large part of your aeroplane's potential if you did not get oxygen as well. If you can get yourself up to somewhere in the twelve to fifteen thousand feet region, and this is possible with many non turbo aeroplanes especially if lightly loaded, the chances are that you will then be above most of the weather and although CBs can easily stretch up to twice that height, you should now be able to see them from miles off as they will no longer be embedded.

IFR approved GPS

At around £8,000 this is an expensive piece of kit. It will do all the clever things that a non approved GPS will do, including a moving map, but the 'approval', which accounts for a major part of the price, buys you RAIM (a self checking facility not found on other sets, which are therefore more liable to mislead you without warning). You will also get IFR approach procedures for many (but not all) airfields and you will be able to add 'R' in the equipment box of your IFR flight plan, which indicates that you are equipped for Basic RNAV and so controllers can and will give you direct routings across continents instead of keeping you plodding along the airways from waypoint to waypoint, navigating by VOR and DME. If you often fly airways, the 'R' is desirable; furthermore, before long, GPS approaches will become available in Europe, but only to those with the 'approved' sets. It will be a pity to be left out of all that but maybe, by the time that GPS approaches have become common in Europe, an 'approved' set will be less costly.

Non-approved GPS

If you are serious about flying as a means of transport, I should regard a decent GPS set as essential. If you can't afford an 'approved' IFR GPS then a non approved set with a good moving map will have to do. The gliding fraternity has spawned freeware for PDAs that provides good moving maps for only a few hundred pounds. In their case they were motivated by competition rules that penalise those who enter CTAs. The gliders carry sealed GPS sets and the judges know exactly where they have been. Sets can also be bought off the shelf and the best in the summer of 2007 seem to be the Flymap at around £600 and the Bendix/King Skymap III at about £1,150. There are better sets for yet more money, but none is 'approved' and none will get you direct routings on the airways nor allow GPS approaches.

VOR/DME shifter

This is an obsolescent piece of kit, probably out of production now, but you can still find a Bendix/King KNS80 or something similar on the second hand market, particularly as they are now being ripped out of aircraft to make room for IFR GPS sets. They have two great virtues: as a poor man's 'approved' GPS alternative and as a very convenient GPS checking system. Many VOR/DME shifters have been approved for BRNAV and thus allow you to enter the magic 'R' in the Equipment box of the IFR flight plan and by this means you can route direct. In practice their limitations are poor range (60 nm from the VOR beacon), poor accuracy (+/- 5 deg.) and an operating system that makes it very easy to set up something quite different from what you wanted. Although not as accurate as GPS they are reasonably accurate within their limitations and if you set up your VOR/DME shifter with the same waypoints as you have in your GPS flight plan, whether it an 'approved' set or not, you will get a constant cross check that your GPS is behaving as it should. In my experience, when the two sets do not agree, in nine times out of ten it is because I have erred in my setting up of the VOR/DME shifter and on the tenth occasion it is because of rubbish entered into the GPS. So far, I have never experienced a GPS set, or any other navigational instrument other than an ADF, offering misleading information: the fault has always been the pilot's but that is still a good reason for always running two navigation systems. However reliable you may think your GPS to be, I can promise you that the operator will always be fallible from time to time. Two systems should protect you against your own inadequacies and, in any case, you are expected to monitor your GPS somehow, even if it is 'approved'. In IMC the only way available is by checking your GPS position against VOR bearings and DME ranges and a VOR/DME shifter will do this for you continually.

I have successfully flown airways as far as Prague and Stockholm with nothing more than a hand held GPS set and a KNS80, giving me the coveted 'R' and a means of checking my GPS. The hand held GPS has always been far more accurate than the KNS80 but the KNS80 has kept me legal, given me confidence in my hand held and also, in my case, provided a second ILS with glideslope that confirms the indications on the primary ILS. That is a useful extra protection for someone who has been known to forget to check glideslope accuracy against DME and altitude readings on an ILS approach.

HSI and flight director

An HSI makes interpretation of what the heading, CDI and ADF indications actually mean more intuitive and a flight director even more so. We can all remember how, during training, we gazed blankly at the dials, flummoxed as to which way to turn to get back on to track. Some of us are still capable of such confusion even now, especially with nothing more than a DI and particularly if somewhat out of practice. An HSI will set you back about £5,000; I have never even inquired about the cost of a flight director, much as I should like to have one; I have managed without either so far. They are both desirable equipment but if you cannot afford them then you will just have to practise more often so as manage well at cross referencing the DI against the navigational indications. If you have to, you can do it and if you are uncomfortable without these optional extras, keep practising on any IFR simulation software until you are confident of being able to cope.

Redundancy

A second alternator and doubling of any other electrical equipment, vacuum pump, attitude indicator, approved GPS or anything else on which you rely at times must be a worthwhile contribution to safety. An electrical failure at night in difficult weather conditions, for instance, could stack up the difficulties beyond your ability to cope, so if you haven't got much redundancy perhaps you should avoid flying at night in difficult weather. However, you can go some way to preparing for equipment failures by working out in advance how you might cope. You already carry a torch when night flying, which is a first step. A hand held battery operated GPS could prove a godsend and even my revalidation examiner agrees that in real life I should be a fool to use the magnetic compass in the event of failure of the DI when the track indication on the GPS is so much easier to use. Some GPS sets even offer a complete virtual panel.

Glass cockpit

If you have got one, you're a lucky pilot, if not you will just have to plod on with what you have got because the cost of a refit is, so far, a good deal more than even the cost of a zero timed engine.

Second engine or a turbine

Provided that you are properly trained and (very important, this) in good current practice, the loss of one engine, when you have two, should be no more than an inconvenience. The chances of a turbine engine ever failing are statistically far less likely than with a piston engine, so, assuming that the pilot is properly trained and current, the piston twin and the turbine are both materially safer than the piston single. You should take account of this deficiency in a single piston when making the go, no go decision. Should you fly IFR when the cloud base is only just above the ground? Should you fly at night? Should you fly over water, especially in Winter? If you do, even in summer, should you make sure that you have a modern locator beacon, a survival suit and a dinghy.

De-icing

This is well beyond the reach of the budget conscious pilot. High power and low weight may whip you up satisfactorily above the icing level before ice defeats you but there are some scenarios, a hold in the freezing layer in a cold soaked airframe for instance, for which de icing would be very welcome. Without it, you must always have some other answer, which usually amounts to practical VFR conditions beneath the cloud base. If the METAR and the TAF don't offer this, don't go.

Thunderstorm detection

Either of the types available seem fairly effective and the cost is moderate. If you fly often in continental Europe, where CBs can be massive, you might well consider fitting one of these. Without one, you will just have to stay on the ground when serious embedded CBs are forecast. In the UK, however, I can recall only one break up of an aeroplane in a CB – a motor glider – and I am personally willing to chance an encounter with a moderate home grown CB but always take good care to see that anything heavy is well tied down. I also keep the speed down in or near a CB to significantly less than Manoeuvring Speed. Curiously, the more lightly loaded you are, the lower should your speed be to avoid overstressing. I should not contemplate flight in even a modest UK CB with any but the most imperturbable of passengers.

TAS

A Traffic Advisory System is one more of those things that would be nice to have if you could afford one, but so would be all sorts of other things. A beautifully varnished steam yacht with a crack crew would be quite nice and so would a flying boat. But some of us will just have to rub along without, depending, when nothing else is available, on the quadrantal or semi circular rule and the bigness of the sky to keep us apart from other IFR traffic. I comfort myself with the thought that during World War II the UK skies were full of uncontrolled traffic, much of it IFR, and yet mid airs in IFR were very rare. They even used to fly formation in cloud. So the chances of an IFR mid air are probably less than they are of being struck by lightning while out for a walk. Do you carry a lightning conductor at all times?

Conclusion

There are, no doubt, other desiderata that I have overlooked, and I apologise for this. If, like me, you cannot afford many of the tempting bits of kit so enthusiastically promoted in the flying magazines that does not have to mean that you need be priced out of the skies. Much more important than having all the bells and whistles is having good reliable steady competence in what you do have. If you are well acquainted with your own kit, minimal thought it may be, and in good practice you are likely to be a more able pilot than the one whose technical competence falls short of his equipment level. Technically advanced aircraft bring with them high risks caused mostly by their owners' exaggerated concept of the weather proofing that the new equipment has brought them. It's exactly the same scenario as car drivers pushing their limits further because they now have anti-locking brakes and air bags. Research by the US AOPA Air Safety Foundation has found that 45% of fatal accidents involving Technically Advanced Aircraft were weather related, as compared with 16% of conventionally equipped aircraft. I find considerable consolation, as well as a substantial cost saving, in continuing to lurk in the 16% bracket.

3   The use of oxygen in general aviation

By Steven Copeland

I am sure that all of us will recall our basic physiology theory from the PPL and various instrument related ground studies? So we will all recall that oxygen is the gas of life! First discovered in 1774 and used in medicine since its discovery it is one of the key elements in the air that we breathe. Air contains 21% oxygen and 70% nitrogen with a few other inert gases thrown in for good measure. Our bodies only metabolise around 4% of the oxygen in the air at each breath (the reason that artificial respiration works).

Hypoxia

So what relevance is this to us aviators? As we all know the higher we go the lower the atmospheric pressure and thus the lower the partial pressure of oxygen. This leads to a condition known as hypoxia. Hypoxia is a reduction of oxygen in the body at a cellular level and occurs when the oxygen content of inhaled air is reduced or the conditions impede the diffusion of O2 from the lungs into the blood stream.

Usually the higher the altitude we go to the shorter the exposure time is before symptoms occur. We also need to take into account an individual's physiological altitude, which can be effected by stress, tobacco and alcohol.

Many high altitude chamber experiments have shown that a person affected by hypoxia may recognize only a fraction of its known indications. In fact, some experienced pilots don't even report experiencing any effects at all while they are obviously incapacitated. This is where the insidious nature of hypoxia is so dangerous. Many pilots blackout or faint in flight each year from hypoxia. In reviewing many of the so-called pilot error deaths and serious accidents, in which no tangible explanation was found for cause, they may in fact have been caused by hypoxia.

At what altitude will I get hypoxia? This is the most difficult question to answer. You can suffer from the effects of hypoxia at almost any altitude where there is a quick altitude gain of about 8,000 feet. Quick in this case is about 150 ft/min. It's the loss of oxygen (pressure) on your body that causes your blood to lose some of its ability to absorb oxygen and possibly out-gas (lose oxygen), resulting in hypoxia.

Many who live at lower altitudes have blood that is conditioned to a point where the oxygen collecting factor is lower than that needed for the altitude gain. This can be compensated by "high altitude conditioning". The mechanism of this conditioning is not well understood, but does seem to work where moderate altitude exposure and exercise are performed. Many proficient pilots have become (somewhat) conditioned through their flying and can withstand more exposure without ill effects.

Fortunately there are number of signs and symptoms that can help us identify hypoxia; from the subjective they include shortness of breath, apprehension, nausea, headache, dizziness, euphoria, belligerence, blurred and tunnel vision, numbness and tingling through to the objective which include hyperventilation, cyanosis, confusion, poor judgement and muscle spasms.

Smokers are particularly prone to the effects of hypoxia and strangely the most adamant as a group that they do not suffer from the effects, perhaps justifying one of the subjective symptoms of belligerence!

As aviators the most important effects of hypoxia are those affecting the nervous system. Nerve tissue has a greater requirement for oxygen and thus brain tissue is the first to be affected by oxygen deficiency. As the brain is starved of oxygen, decision-making is impaired and the brain starts to shut down leading to unconsciousness and even death. The time that we have to take corrective action is referred to as the time of useful consciousness and is the time available from the interruption of oxygen to take corrective action to the time when the ability to take corrective action is lost.

The table below shows the approximate time of useful consciousness.

Altitude (feet)	Progressive Decompression (Inactive)	Progressive Decompression (Moderate Activity)	Rapid Decompression
18,000	40 min	30 min	20 min
20,000	10 min	5 min	3 min
25,000	5 min	3 min	2 min
30,000	1.5 min	45 sec	30 sec
35,000	45 sec	30 sec	20 sec

| 40,000 | 25 sec | 18 sec | 12 sec |
| 43,000 | 18 sec | 12 sec | 12 sec |

As you can see the higher you go or the more rapid the decompression the shorter the useful time available to you to rectify the situation.

The effects of hypoxia present in several different stages, the first is the indifferent stage, this is the effect of mild hypoxia with night vision being affected at around 4,000ft.

This is followed by the compensatory stage where the circulatory system and to a lesser degree the respiratory system provide a defence against hypoxia. Pulse rate, blood pressure, cardiac output and respiration rate all increase in an attempt to compensate. But even with the best efforts of our bodies after 10-15 minutes exposure impaired efficiency is obvious.

Next is the disturbance stage with vision diminished, weakness and loss of muscular coordination, sensation of touch and pain are diminished and hearing starts to be affected. Thinking slows down and short-term memory is affected and the skin and nail beds can take on a blue tinge due to cyanosis (a bluish or purplish skin colour caused by the presence of high levels of deoxygenated haemoglobin in blood vessels near the skin surface. It occurs when the oxygen saturation level falls below 85-90%).

Finally there is the critical stage; within five minutes judgement and co-ordination deteriorate and finally dizziness and the unconsciousness occur. Not an ideal situation to be in when in command of an aircraft!

Use of oxygen in general aviation

So what are the guidelines for use of oxygen? Until recently there were no official guidelines or legal requirement to use oxygen for those of us operating under CAA regulations. Following a change to the ANO in 2007 we are now required to use oxygen above FL100 for that part of the flight where the duration is greater than 30 minutes. FL100 to FL130 oxygen is to be used by all the flight crew and above FL130 all passengers are recommended to use oxygen. The standards can be found in Annex 6 Part II for those interested!

Personal experience shows 14,000 feet as being a good point to consider putting passengers onto oxygen and definitely at 15,000 feet and above.

For those of you operating under the US system the FAA is a little more prescriptive in the recommendations for the use of oxygen.

FAR 91.211 - Un-pressurized Aircraft*

Altitude	Oxygen requirement
Less than 12,500 ft	None
Above 12,500 ft up to 14,000 ft	Crew only if more than 30 minutes
Above 14,000 ft up to 15,000 ft	Crew only at all times
Above 15,000 ft	Crew and passengers at all times

* Also for cabin pressure altitude in pressurized airplanes

So that's all the doom and gloom out of the way, as pilots the question is what can we do to prevent the effects of hypoxia? The answer is very simple; we take our own with us! There are a wide variety of systems available ranging from simple constant flow mechanical systems to advanced electronic systems that give vast durations from small lightweight cylinders.

Cylinders

As with most things aviation, the majority of systems and cylinders come from the United States. This brings a number of compatibility issues for cylinder filling and testing. The US use a set of standards developed by the compressed gas association and the standard used for oxygen is the CGA-540 thread. In Europe we have our own standards known as DIN and the oxygen fitting is a DIN477-9. So filling US cylinders requires an adaptor not often available at gas filling stations. It is here another problem appears in that under European regulations a filling station may not fill a cylinder that does not carry a European hydrostatic test stamp and a CE mark.

Many holders of US specification cylinders have been able to get them filled and in the past even get them tested in Europe, but the future of this procedure is not clear at the moment. Fortunately it is possible to get European specification cylinders with US specification valves or even get the US kits with native European threads, which can then be mated to the appropriate approved cylinder.

There are other advantages to using European specification cylinders apart from easier filling; the working pressure is much higher allowing us to use smaller cylinders at higher pressure to give the same volumes of gas. Obviously a major weight saving can be gained in a light aircraft by using these smaller high-pressure cylinders. The type of cylinder can also be a factor when looking at weight saving with steel, aluminium and carbon cylinders being readily available. At the lightest end of the scale are carbon Kevlar® cylinders but these are also the most expensive costing upwards of several hundred pounds.

Oxygen refilling

The gas that goes into the cylinder also comes in different grades or more specifically what gets delivered to your door comes in different grades. All oxygen whether used for medical, welding, diving or aviation is produced in the same manner and delivered from the same 'tap' at the gas company. The differences in grades are down to differences in cylinder preparation. Aviation, medical or diving grade oxygen is dried and dedicated cylinders are used which are completely vacuumed before filling, every cylinder is then individually tested and tagged. Other grades of gas are generally not dried and any available cylinder is used (often being re-sprayed after filling to meet gas marking standards) with no vacuuming and only a percentage of cylinders tested. This means that a cylinder used for another gas such as argon or neon or something much more unfriendly could then be cross-filled with oxygen leading to a contaminated fill and delivered without being tested.

There is also a temptation by pilots to fill their own cylinders. Not a problem for those who have been trained in the safe handling of high-pressure oxygen and are using correctly cleaned oxygen-safe filling equipment. But it is very easy to contaminate filling equipment, turn the gas on too quickly and whoosh! You suddenly you have completed all three side of the fire triangle with remarkable results!

Oxygen delivery

The variety of methods for actually delivering the oxygen to the pilot is as diverse as the choice of cylinder we store the gas in. Many prefer to use an electronic demand system from Mountain High designated the O2D2 which sounds like something out of Star Wars! This is a two-place unit that monitors the user's breathing cycle and provides oxygen through a cannula on demand. The advantage of this type of unit over a constant flow unit is a vastly improved duration of supply. As an example, an O2D2 kit with a 2 litre carbon fibre cylinder weighs in at a very lightweight 3lbs for the entire kit and provides a 30 man hour duration. A similar constant flow kit providing the same duration weighs in at close to 25lbs. Relying on electronics has its own problems as an electronic or battery failure potentially leaves you without oxygen. There are a number of ways to mitigate this; for example, you can carry spare constant flow cannulae that can be plugged into the same unit but looking at it practically, there are very few places flying in Europe other than over the Alps where we could not descend to safe altitude immediately and still be above MSA.

Another important consideration is the ability to check that in addition to delivery of the gas the kit is actually doing it's job and maintaining your oxygen saturation levels. The pulse oxymeter is the simplest way of checking this. This is a safe and simple medical device that that provides non-invasive and continuous information about the percentage of oxygen that is combined with haemoglobin. It detects and calculates the absorption of light by oxygenated blood to produce a measurement called SpO_2, an estimate of oxygen saturation.

Whatever our chosen method of delivery one thing is clear, when we are flying un-pressurised light aircraft; carrying oxygen improves our safety and increases our operating ability. If you take good care of yourself and eat well you will be able to withstand and tolerate more altitude exposure with less effects and recover from any oxygen deficiency faster. If you use oxygen, you will be adding invaluable insurance to your safety, health and sense of well-being.

4 Transitioning to a glass cockpit

By Anthony Bowles

After flying a Grumman Tiger for some 20 years, last year I bought a Cirrus SR22, a modern aircraft with an all glass cockpit. This article is a personal reflection on the transition process from a conventionally equipped light aircraft.

First, why that choice? My Grumman Tiger had served me well and for its time had reasonable avionics, which I had upgraded to a point. However to bring the aircraft into the 21st century from an avionics viewpoint would have required substantial expenditure; in addition the engine had done about 1,500 hours since its last overhaul and so would also need major work in the not so distant future. In addition, very strong headwinds on a number of my "milk run" Carlisle to Elstree trips last autumn made me yearn for something usefully faster and participation in the **PPL/IR Europe** trips to Greece (2005) and Tunisia/Sicily (2006) had demonstrated the advantages of aircraft with longer range than the Tiger. All these factors, combined with a feeling that I had time for one more aircraft in my flying life, led me to decide to investigate a change in aircraft.

Cirrus SR22

Initially I was quite taken with a Trinidad but decided that the incremental increase in cruise speed would not justify the substantial costs involved in any change. Some suggested a Mooney but I was put off by their dislike of grass strips and the lack of any UK dealership. There was no Cessna or Piper aircraft that interested me and so I turned my attention to the Cirrus and Columbia designs. A requirement that any aircraft needed to be EASA certifiable quickly ruled out the Columbia and that left the Cirrus. An SR20 would give me around an additional 25 Kts cruise while an SR22 would add 35-40 Kts depending on power settings. The SR22 looked tempting.

And so one early November 2006 day saw me taxying out at Turweston for my first Cirrus experience. A second followed a couple of weeks later to explore IMC flying, holds and ILS approaches followed by a visit to RGV at Gloucester, which is the main Cirrus maintenance organisation in the UK, to suss out what the engineers thought of the aircraft. I was hoping to acquire a pre-owned SR22 but at that stage there were only three on the UK register and while with time, I probably could have sourced a suitable N reg pre-owned model and put it on the UK register, I decided to "bite the bullet" and buy new. This would have the advantage of avoiding the unsatisfactory way that ADF and DME had been installed in some European Cirrus aircraft. The latest version of the Primary Flight Display (PFD) software allows ADF bearings to be displayed as a RMI on the HSI display rather than through a separate, obsolete, RBI indicator.

Having reached the Cirrus choice through a somewhat negative path of ruling out other possibilities, once I tried out the aircraft, my reaction was immensely positive. The large PFD straight in front of my vision with horizon above and HSI below with speed and altitude tapes on either side seemed immediately intuitive. The PFD displays much other information as well and I come back to this shortly.

Transition training

Purchase of a new Cirrus includes transition training which in the UK is done by TAA UK based at Denham. Delays in my aircraft being ready meant that my training took place on a TAA aircraft and on a particularly windy day in March 2007, Rob McNay from TAA duly turned up at Turweston to do my training. Late the following day, Rob signed me off; while I felt competent in the basic handling of the aircraft, I could not claim to feel entirely at home yet, particularly with the minutiae of the dual Garmin 430s of which I had no previous experience.

Two weeks later, son Humphrey flew the Tiger down to her new owners at Biggin Hill with me enjoying a rare moment as passenger and an hour or so later, we flew back to Carlisle in my new SR22. It was a lovely day like much of April last year; Humphrey had flown down VFR and I filed IFR for the return journey. We climbed effortlessly to FL100 and even against a 20 kt headwind, with a ground speed around 150 Kts I could see that my milk run was about to enter a new era of speedy comfort. Now some 150 plus hours later, I feel more competent on giving a view on transition to a glass cockpit.

Glass cockpit

The PFD replaces the traditional "six pack" so that instead of scanning six dials, you look at one picture on the PFD. Not quite true because in the panel bolster, there are three conventional instruments – ASI, AH and Altimeter – for backup use in the event of a PFD failure. I find the airspeed and altimeter tapes easy to assimilate and on each side of the artificial horizon ideally placed. In turbulent air, the ASI varies much more than the damped mechanical instrument which initially can be a little disconcerting and encourage "speed chasing". The balance indicator is a small triangle at the top of the artificial horizon while a small blue semi-circular tape appears just above the HSI to indicate a rate one turn in the appropriate direction. The VSI is just to the right of the altimeter tape and replicates the mechanical instrument through a 90° arc; a centrally placed needle indicates straight and level flight; it moves clockwise to indicate a climb and anti-clockwise to indicate a descent.

There is much space left on the panel to display other data. To the left of the ASI tape is a percentage power tape computed from engine RPM and manifold pressure. I soon got used to the idea of setting a certain percentage power from the engine rather than by reference to adjustments to engine RPM and manifold pressure - there is no manual variable propeller pitch control in the Cirrus. Along the top of the display are various autopilot configuration annunciations showing at a glance autopilot state.

The lower half of the PFD is given over to the HSI display; this can be configured to show either a 360° or 120° compass rose with or without mapping at selectable ranges. Selection is a question of user preference; with a moving map available on the MFD (multi function display), I prefer an uncluttered view so use a 360° display with no moving map. The CDI bar on the HSI can be linked to either of the two GPS or VOR receivers via the NAV switch to the left of the HSI. Additionally, a RMI can be displayed linked to either GPS or VOR receiver or (in my aircraft) to the ADF via the bearing switch. A third aux switch allows the digital display of any data switchable to the RMI. Where a GPS input is selected on any switch, then bearing, distance and time to waypoint is displayed; any other input gives bearing only.

To the left and below the HSI, a rectangular box displays TAS, GS and OAT. A similar box below and to the right of the HSI displays engine RPM, manifold pressure, oil pressure and fuel flow. Above and to the right of the HSI, there is a wind vector arrow with digital readout of GPS computed wind direction and speed. To the right side of the HSI are various switches for selecting the heading bug, target/cleared altitude/flight level, VSI climb and descent rates and altimeter pressure settings.

Much of the additional data mentioned in the last paragraph is available (at least in theory) in conventional cockpits either directly by delving into the relevant pages of the GPS receiver or indirectly through appropriate manipulation of the old circular aviation slide rule. But there is simply nothing to beat the clarity of this data presentation on the PFD, and in particular, the graphical presentation of relative wind. A nice addition to the HSI is a dotted GPS computed trend line which with the adjacent relative wind graphic should allow for perfect tracking acquisition and maintenance.

Selecting an ILS navigation input activates a soft switch to allow appropriate bearing selection for the CDI which works in conventional mode. Additionally small horizontal and vertical displays appear below and to the right of the AH; some criticize the lack of vertical guidance adjacent to the HSI as is found in conventional mechanical units but I have found placing the vertical guidance on the same scanning line as the AH, altimeter tape and VSI pointer logical.

Map display

As a multi function display (MFD) implies, a variety of data can be shown on this screen, centrally placed in a Cirrus. For most of the time, the moving map will be selected fed by either of the GPS receivers. User preference determines whether a topographical display is selected, coastline/political features only or no geographical information. Except in mountainous areas where I find a full topographical display helpful, I prefer to have a basic coastline/political features display which presents an uncluttered and thus easy to read screen. The user must decide on whether to have a north up, track up or heading up display and then select the appropriate range. The range selected will determine the extent of the aeronautical information shown. On my Cirrus, I find that a 50 to 100 nm range is convenient for cruise while a 20 to 30 mile range suits departure and arrival phases. If you prefer, the moving map can be configured to give a 120° arc forward view.

My Cirrus is equipped with both stormscope and Skywatch traffic system and data from these units is overlaid on the moving map. If you are flying a flight plan stored in the GPS receiver, then this is also overlaid on the map with the active leg shown in magenta. Changes to routing initiated by the "direct to" button on the Garmin 430 are echoed to the MFD. Data boxes at the top left and right hand side of the moving map display show graphical readouts of engine CHT and EGTs, oil temperature and pressure, GS and miles to run and ETAs for the next waypoint and destination. The colour of the data shown is also important; green if all looks good, yellow indicates a cautionary value requiring monitoring and red indicates a possible problem requiring attention.

On start up after the fuel loading page, the MFD displays the engine data page which displays all engine data parameters, and in addition shows density altitude, OAT, fuel consumption in absolute terms and as miles per US gallon. A small niggle for me is that although litres can be selected as a unit of fuel quantity for fuel addition purposes, all fuel calculations remain based on US gallon units. I use the engine data display page for taxying and departure, and for using the lean assist function when leaning the mixture for the cruise.

Jeppesen charts

Other pages available depend to some extent on options selected at purchase time; my Cirrus has TAWS but so far I have not found much occasion to use this, a trip page where details of ETAs and fuel remaining at each waypoint are continuously updated, a nearest page for airports, VORs, NDBs etc which can then be used to find relevant frequencies and display basic landing information, various electronic checklists, which I personally do not normally use, set up pages which allow some personal tailoring of data displayed and finally but by no means least, the CMax pages for display of airfield instrument charts providing one has the relevant subscription from Jeppesen. The approach charts are geo-referenced with your aeroplane shown in green on the relevant chart and a nice feature is that on landing, the approach chart switches to the airport ground chart, again geo-referenced, which makes taxiing around strange airports much easier.

It took me a while to fathom out how all these various functions worked; I was greatly helped by Cirrus/RGV setting up the MFD with the usual default settings for UK/European use and I have only made one or two minor changes since. In terms of easing workload and general safety, a large moving map display is an enormous benefit, particularly for VFR navigation round congested airspace where likewise the Skywatch traffic system comes into its own providing instant bearing and relative height information on nearby transponding aircraft.

System failures

So what happens when the music stops and the PFD and MFD go blank? Rob delighted in mischievously pulling the relevant circuit breakers during my training. Conditions were VMC at the time and reversion to the bolster instruments was quite straightforward although I would prefer them to be somewhat higher placed in the cockpit. The autopilot still functions in GPSS mode if the PFD goes down, and navigation is still possible using GPS or VOR with the corresponding Garmin 430 visual display. If IMC, then I would certainly wish to get into VMC as quickly as possible. Height hold or climb/descent at preset rates is also possible with the S-TEC 55 autopilot.

In some ways loss of all engine information on a PFD/MFD display may be somewhat more disconcerting, certainly when one's experience on the aircraft in question is limited and you have yet to master exactly what a particular power setting gives in terms of aircraft performance. The Garmin 430 has a mapping display albeit much more limited due to small screen size. Loss of CMax chart information emphasises the need for carrying paper charts for your intended destination and alternates.

I have no experience of the Garmin 1000 EFIS; I understand failure of one unit allows the other unit to be switched to PFD or MFD mode as appropriate but failure of both units (perhaps very unlikely) does mean no backup at all while dual failure of the Avidyne displays fitted in the Cirrus still leaves you with basic communication and navigation facilities using the Garmin 430s.

Garmin GNS430

While the Garmin 430 units can feature in any aircraft with modern avionics, glass cockpit or not, they are certainly worth a separate paragraph in this article. My previous experience with a panel mounted IFR unit was limited to a much simpler piece of kit and I found it took considerable manual reading and experimentation before I felt entirely comfortable with their operation, and even now I am sure there are some utilities that I have yet to explore. Having a dual installation does provide a pleasing element of redundancy as well as utility in being able to store additional flight plans and display two different flight modes simultaneously. I normally have the top 430 set to the default NAV page (data to next way point) and the lower 430 to the map page unless I need access to one of the less used other pages. The crossfill utility enables copying of all user supplied data (flight plans, user way points etc) from one unit to the other.

ADF and DME

I added two extras to my Cirrus, both necessary for IFR flight in the UK. First was a King KR87 ADF which via a Sandel converter unit displays bearing information on the PFD. There is much debate on various web fora on the aeronautical (as opposed to legal) need for this but I think NDB approaches will be around for a while in Europe. The second extra was a KN63 DME unit with its display to the right of the MFD just above the ADF box in place of the glove box and where the old analogue engine instruments are in older cirri.

Glass cockpits are increasingly appearing in new aircraft and will be increasingly available for retrofit in older aircraft. The information that can be displayed on an electronic display is astonishingly detailed and has great advantages for flight safety for both VFR and IFR flight. In transitioning to a glass cockpit environment, one must understand the limitations and potential failure consequences of such an environment but most pilots will make the transition with ease.

What have I most missed from my Grumman? A good place to put my old fashioned stop watch. There are four different electronic timers in my SR22 but there is nothing to beat a traditional stop watch for hold and other timings; I have recently found a moderately suitable place adjacent to the flap switch – not ideal but just within scanning range.

After note: Columbia Aircraft have since been taken over by Cessna with their aircraft rebranded as top of the piston engine range Cessna aircraft. I would expect EASA certification for these in time.

SECTION 3

Operational Matters

Section Contents

1 Self-flown GA IFR transport in Europe: a user's guide

By Vasa Babic

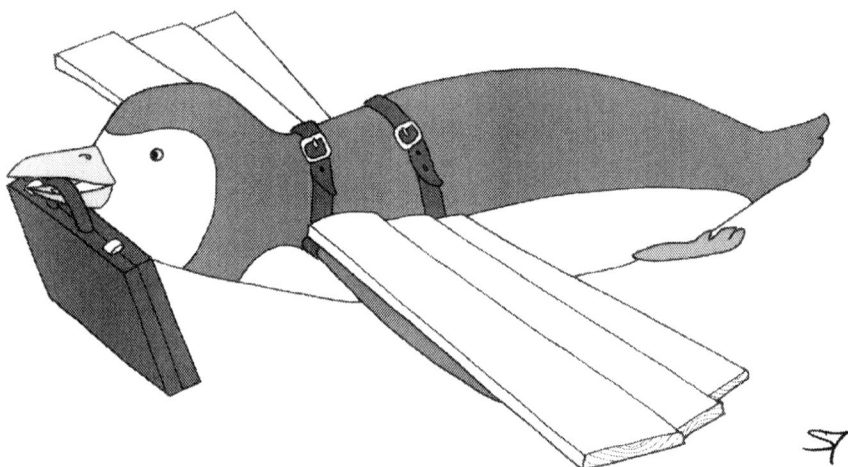

Much of the time and effort we put into GA IFR is ultimately about transport; being able to go places more safely and reliably than under VFR, faster than by surface transport and more flexibly than airline schedules permit. During the last year, my GA flying met two distinct, travel-related criteria for the first time:

- A relatively large number of sectors (50) were flown to meet personal or business transport requirements which determined the destination and timing. These were mostly routes from the south of England to major European international airports, where the only alternative to flying myself would have been airline travel or a business charter. The 50 sectors do not include training and currency flights, short trips between smaller GA airfields or travel where a major part of the purpose was flying rather than getting there (e.g. a cross-channel lunch in France, or a touring trip across Europe).

- All of my European air travel was self-flown; the only airline flights I took were long-haul ones.

This article summarises my experience over these 50 sectors; to review how effective GA was as a mode of transport, and to provide elements of a "how-to guide" for the less experienced IFR pilot. The aircraft used was a Cessna 421C, a six-eight seat pressurised piston twin with known-ice certification.

The 50 sectors were flown between the aircraft's base at Bournemouth [EGHH] and 20 different destinations (a few were repeated). Three sectors were fuel stops, so the total was 47 actual point-point legs; a

Figure 1. Average flight time and airways distances

Destinations		Month	No. of sectors
LYBE	Belgrade	January	0
LEBL	Barcelona	February	2
EGSC	Cambridge	March	3
LFMD	Cannes	April	13
EGNC	Carlisle	May	6
EGPN	Dundee	June	7
LSGG	Geneva	July	7
EGPF	Glasgow	August	5
EFHF	Helsinki	September	0
LEIB	Ibiza	October	0
EGJJ	Jersey	November	4
LFPB	Le Bourget	December	3
LPPT	Lisbon		
LEMH	Menorca		
ENGM	Oslo	**Summary**	
LEPA	Palma	Sectors	50
LIRZ	Perugia	Average airborne time	2.5hrs
EHAM	Schiphol	Average airways distance	470nm
LFTZ	St Tropez	Average block speed	188kt
LSZH	Zurich		

few of the trips involved multiple legs to more than one destination. Statistically, I've treated them as 25 simple round trips.

The mix of personal and business travel was about half and half. In almost every case, there was little or no time flexibility in the schedule (e.g. I needed to arrive outbound on a given evening and return home the next evening).

In Figure 1, the average flight time and airways distance are estimates based on logged time minus 0.1hrs and great circle distance plus 10%. The average block speed of 188 Kts was achieved with typical true airspeeds of 150 Kts in the climb, 200 Kts cruise and 220 Kts in the descent. Cruise levels were FL140-170 below 400nm and FL180-240 above.

The distances flown were fairly evenly distributed from 100nm-1,000nm. There is a small distortion in Figure 2, because six of the points in the 400-600nm range represent three legs of approximately 1,000nm in which a fuel stop was made.

Figure 2. Distribution of flights according to distance

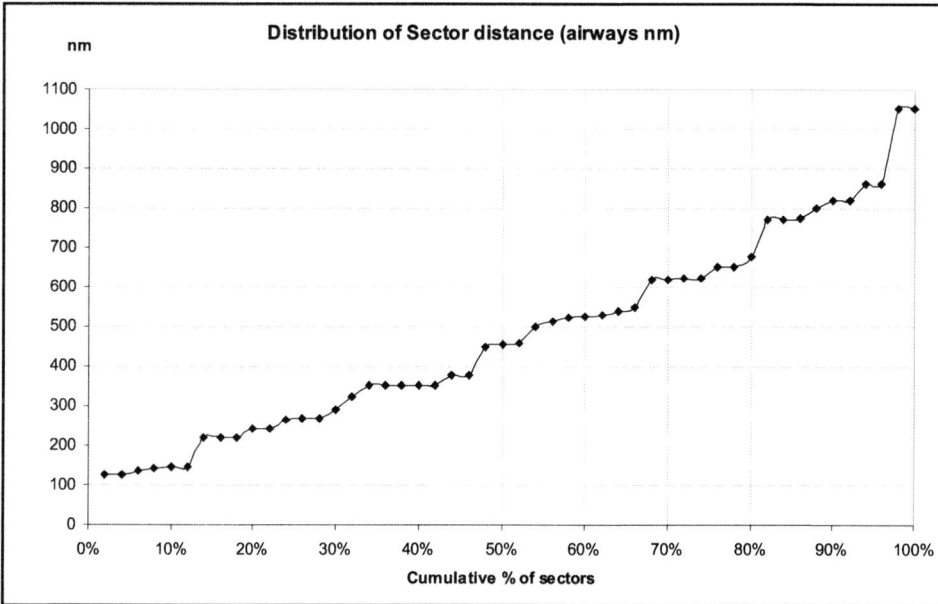

2. Overall Reliability: how practical was it to plan on going places by GA IFR?

I think Figure 3 is one of the most interesting results from this set of data. It shows that of 50 IFR sectors, only one was subject to a major delay and a further six were delayed one-three hours. 43 sectors (86%) arrived within 30mins of the planned time.
I'll describe the delays in some detail, to illustrate the kind of issues than can arise.

Weather
Sector five was a return flight from Cannes [LFMD] to Bournemouth, departing late afternoon. There was a forecast band of thunderstorms running across southern France, and I planned to try and find a way through using weather radar and stormscope. This did not prove possible; I gave up and returned to Cannes after about 30mins outbound and completed the flight the next morning. Half a business day was lost as a result; the alternative would have been to take an evening airline flight from Nice to London and to recover the aircraft later.

Sector 43 involved a two hour delay returning from La Mole-St Tropez [LFTZ] on a bank holiday Monday. The airport has a wind limit of 15 Kts (due to terrain-induced wind shear) and the wind was above limits for almost all of the day. We were able to depart during a brief lull in the late afternoon, because four passengers and I had waited at the airport ready to go; few other aircraft left that day.

ATC

Sector three was a departure from Perugia [LIRZ] in Umbria, about 150km NW of Rome. Some slow airport bureaucracy when paying for fuel and landing fees and slot led to a one hour delay. In general, I received very few airways slot times (never more than a 30mins delay) and no en-route or arrival delays. I only flew holds once, for about 10mins, when I arrived at St Gallen whilst it was closed for lunch. Barcelona, Palma, Helsinki, Schiphol and Zurich were the destinations requiring airport slots, but I used commercial handlers in each case, and they managed the process so that I never experienced any arrival or departure time restriction.

Ground Delay

The Sector 17 delay of two hours at Belgrade [LYBE] was due to a convoluted process of paying fees, flight planning, fuelling and de-icing that involved two escorted trips through main terminal security and to and from the aircraft. A dedicated GA terminal opened at Belgrade a few months later and this process is now fast and convenient.

All the remaining ground delays related solely to avgas refuelling. The 1.5hrs in Sector 32 was due to repositioning from Helsinki Vantaa [EFHK], the main commercial airport which did not have avgas, to the nearby Helsinki Malmi [EFHF], the GA airport which did, but which was closed at the time I arrived the previous day.

The two hour delay in Sector 33 was because I had to stop for fuel at Lelystad [EHLE] on an Oslo [ENGM] to Bournemouth leg. Despite confirming the availability of avgas at Oslo, the bowser ran dry whilst I was fuelling, and no delivery was available for several days.

Figure 3. Experience of delays

Sector	Wx	ATC	Ground
1	None	None	None
2	None	None	None
3	None	None	None
4	None	0.5 hrs	0.5 hrs
5	12 hrs	None	None
6	None	None	None
7	None	None	None
8	None	None	None
9	None	None	None
10	None	None	None
11	None	None	None
12	None	None	None
13	None	None	None
14	None	None	None
15	None	None	None
16	None	None	None
17	None	None	2 hrs
18	None	None	None
19	None	None	None
20	None	None	None
21	None	None	None
22	None	None	None
23	None	None	None
24	None	None	None
25	None	None	None
26	None	None	None
27	None	None	None
28	None	None	None
29	None	None	None
30	None	None	None
31	None	None	None
32	None	None	1.5 hrs
33	None	None	2 hrs
34	None	None	None
35	None	None	None
36	None	None	None
37	None	None	None
38	None	None	None
39	None	None	None
40	None	None	None
41	None	None	None
42	None	None	None
43	2 hrs	None	None
44	None	None	None
45	None	None	None
46	None	None	None
47	None	None	None
48	None	None	None
49	None	None	None
50	None	None	3 hrs

The Sector 50 delay was at Palma de Majorca, at a peak time for airline departures, when the sole avgas supplier was too busy to serve the GA apron for a couple of hours.

Maintenance

There were no maintenance-related cancellations or delays, or periods the aircraft was unavailable other than a three -week annual inspection. The interim 50hr inspections and ad hoc defect work were conducted between planned flights.

I'll discuss each of these factors in more detail below, but, overall, I think the statistics are representative of what is achievable in this kind of operation. I think it was a good year for weather and maintenance, offset by some delays (Belgrade, Palma and Perugia) that were down to inexperience and which I could avoid in the future.

3. The IMC experience: weather encountered

The following is a summary of weather-related statistics for the 50 sectors, they are my estimates based on memory and logbook records of instrument flight time.

Flight in IMC

I found it quite surprising how little actual IMC was encountered:

- 12% of the flight time took place in IMC (i.e. an average of 18mins per 2.5hr sector).

- Only six sectors (12%) had more than 30mins in IMC.

The 50 sectors were somewhat concentrated in spring/summer (see Figure 1), but the worst weather encountered, by far, were thunderstorms over the French Alps in summer and frontal weather in the UK in June.

Instrument Approaches

Every sector terminated at an airport with a published instrument approach procedure, however most approaches were flown entirely in VMC:

- 17 out of 50 (34%) encountered IMC beyond the initial approach fix.

- Eight of these (12%) involved a ceiling below 1,000ft.

- Two of these (4%) involved a ceiling below 500ft.

None of the 50 sectors resulted in a missed approach or diversion, and only one required changing a planned destination because of forecast weather – this was a fuel stop that made no difference to the overall journey. In fact, one period of several months involved my flying so little actual IMC (and no "real" approaches) that I needed to do a day of FNPT2 simulator training to keep current.

Icing

Even given the fairly low incidence of IMC, surprisingly little ice was encountered:

⌢ 25 sectors (50%) involved some flight in visible moisture at an OAT of +5°C or less.

⌢ 12 sectors (24%) resulted in some visible traces of airframe ice.

⌢ Six sectors (12%) resulted in ice that could be heard impacting the fuselage from the prop-deice, and the un-heated P2 windshield becoming iced over.

⌢ No sectors required activation of the surface de-ice boots.

Since almost all the cruise flight was above FL160, only a small fraction of the lower level en-route weather was encountered, during the climb and descent. At these cruise levels, icing did seem fairly "binary": it was either trace icing which could be managed indefinitely using only pitot heat and prop deice, or, on a few occasions, rapid icing near a CB which needed immediate avoidance.

Turbulence

No significant turbulence was encountered, except momentarily during storm avoidance. Most of the 12% of flight time that took place in IMC was 'averagely bumpy'; ok for a typical passenger, but enough to worry an anxious one. A couple of sectors experienced 10-20mins of light clear air turbulence. The departure from La Mole, in winds just below the airport limit, encountered enough wind shear to firmly convince me that the limit was not an overly conservative one.

Storms

A significant minority of flights had some form of CB forecast or probable along the route, but I estimate that:

⌢ Only five sectors (10%) required an ATC deviation for weather avoidance, four in the cruise and one in the approach phase.

⌢ For two of these, the avoidance was in VMC.

⌢ For another two, the avoidance was in IMC and based entirely on radar and stormscope data.

⌢ In the final case, avoidance was not possible, and a return to the departure airport was made.

Most of these cases involved entering some bumpy but not hazardous conditions. There were a few other occasions in which I requested non-essential avoidance to make the flight smoother, but would have been prepared to fly through the weather if necessary. ATC are unfailingly helpful in these situations. I think it is fair to distinguish between essential and preferred avoidance when making a request; and to avoid the latter in a busy zone. CB tops are routinely above FL300 and sometimes above FL400. The altitude capability of an advanced piston aircraft like the 421C does not get you over CBs, but it does sometimes make avoidance easier, if you can climb above the layer CBs are embedded in and steer around them visually.

Night flight
All the night flying (one hour after sunset to one hour before sunrise) took place from November to March. Of the total 50 sectors and 125hrs:

- Night flight time was 14hrs (11%) over nine sectors (14%), of which four (8%) where wholly at night;

- Most of the night sectors encountered 10-20mins IMC, one 1.5hr sector was wholly in IMC.

Of the 13 sectors and 25hrs during Nov-March:

- 56% of hours, 30% of take-offs and 70% of landings were at night

To regain currency prior to the first of these night sectors (with four passengers), I found it useful to do a short solo night IFR trip to Jersey and back, so that I practised cruise flight and two ILS approaches at night, rather than just the three full stop landings required. A few brief circuits would not have let me properly check all the aircraft, cabin and panel lighting or get fully comfortable with the aircraft at night.

Weather planning
The WAFC/ICAO FL100-450 Europe Sig Wx chart, Spot Wind charts and TAFs are all that I found necessary for weather planning. No adverse, unforecast weather was encountered. As mentioned above, one fuel stop did require a diversion, and one trip diverted back to its origin due to thunderstorms. Both these outcomes were predicted by the forecasts used.

- Sig Wx Charts generally proved very accurate in terms of regional patterns of cloud and weather. Cloud tops were occasionally understated. The icing and turbulence forecasts are not specific enough to be meaningful. The key item I look for is forecasts of CBs.

- Spot Wind Charts were broadly accurate, and I found long sectors flight times could be planned with 5% or better accuracy. The wind at individual points, observed by air data computer, varied a fair amount from the forecast (by 30 degrees and/or 30% of speed) but always seemed to even out over a sector.

⌒ TAFs proved conservative much of the time, but actual conditions varied from "quite a lot better" to "slightly worse" than forecast. I follow the FAA rules for destination and alternate weather planning, and find them efficient and safe in practice.

I spend no more than a few minutes weather planning for >90% of trips. For a morning flight, I check 24hr TAFs, Sig Wx and Spot Winds the night before, and then get the nine hour TAFs before departure. For an afternoon or evening flight, I do the first stage in the morning – the charts are available only 12hrs in advance. A large band of "FREQ" CBs on the Sig Wx forecast or TAFs below minima are the only potential no-go items, since I have not found en-route ice or turbulence that are beyond the aircraft's legal and practical capabilities, except in CBs. Storms in Europe are usually "ISOL" or "OCNL" and thus adequately spaced for avoidance. I don't really use the various multi-day forecasts or websites, because I don't find they can predict the relatively rare "no-go" weather conditions with any useful specificity.

4. The IMC experience: avionics systems

Storm avoidance

The aircraft is equipped with digital colour weather radar and a stormscope, both displayed on a Honeywell KMD540 multi-function display. They proved useful on a number of sectors, but only essential on two or three.

WX 500 stormscope

This is an excellent device, and I have found its "false negative" error rate to be close to zero – i.e. avoiding the strikes indicated on the display does avoid any dangerous weather, although you may fly through some pretty heavy rain and turbulence that does not generate electrical discharges the instrument can detect. It is subject to "false positive" errors, and at ranges of 40nm or below will display the odd flash where there is no weather hazard. At 80nm or above, the accuracy is erratic – repeated and/or concentrated strikes are a very good indication of a storm, but I've had a number of occasions where either a scattering of strikes around the GPS route overlay at a range of 80-160nm did not prove to be anything but light cloud, or real storms popped-up at 40nm distance in what had previously been strike-free air.

Of course, this could be consistent with the lifecycle of storms forming and dissipating, but my impression is that above 40-80nm, the stormscope is of limited use in planning your route except when it shows very many strikes or none at all. If fuel and other contingencies permit, I would always get closer to anything other than a fairly solid band of strikes, to see how the picture develops at a nearer, but still safe, distance. At ranges of 40nm or closer, the stormscope is very good for tactical avoidance.

Weather radar

One can read weather radar articles about echo properties, masking, attenuation, tilt geometry etc. that make the technology seem rather arcane and difficult. No IFR pilot should be put off by this. I found that, after a little experience, the complexity can be reduced to two basic operating rules:

 Set the tilt to five degrees up

 Don't fly near any yellow or red echoes

Like the stormscope, the weather radar has a range of up to 160nm. However, I found the accuracy even more strongly subject to range. Within 40nm, the radar displays the plan position of heavy rain (in green) and intense rain associated with thunderstorms (in yellow and red) very accurately. Beyond 80nm, I found it pretty useless – you get some dots here and there, but nothing you can use for route planning. This experience is based on fairly isolated cells 5-20nm across, so it may be that larger, intense weather systems do show up clearly at longer range (unless masked by nearer echoes).

Comparison of radar and stormscope

You really need to fly with these systems in visual conditions that let you see the weather and storms they are identifying, and then in IMC, to get a sense of the avoidance margins and tactics that will work safely. I found a handful of flights in the right "teach yourself" conditions hugely valuable.

Radar is better for precision avoidance, especially with storms in the vicinity of an airport, because the depiction is very clear in the horizontal plane and the intensity colour-coding is accurate (to the extent that I've found all-green areas acceptable to fly through, although best avoided with nervous passengers). However, I have once or twice seen a nasty vertical development that had a strike depicted in its centre but no radar echo at all, so I think that using radar exclusively might lead to a very occasional unpleasant encounter that a stormscope would help avoid. However, a stormscope is less precise and has more false warnings, so your avoidance will be more conservative; it might also lead you through dramatic (but safe) heavy rain.

A stormscope is the less expensive and more practical installation, and either system will work well for most GA IFR needs. I have read many vigorous debates between pilots who prefer one system or the other, and I have to conclude that there is real value in having both; in being able to correlate the two displays and in terms of redundancy.

TCAS and EGPWS

The aircraft is fitted with the Honeywell IHAS8000 traffic and terrain avoidance systems. These include audio warnings (e.g. "pull-up", "traffic, traffic") and the MFD reverts to the display mode of the alerting system from any other selected mode.

TCAS is a back-up to ATC radar separation, so it provides 'interesting' rather than critical traffic awareness during routine IFR. It is very useful during low-level VFR in busy parts of the south of England, even though only aircraft with active transponders are detected. It helps you monitor and see converging aircraft more easily than an ATC call of "traffic left to right X o'clock", and is, in effect, a personal airborne SSR display. The system is expensive, so not realistic for most light aircraft, but if one's budget can stretch to it, TCAS does not disappoint. I chose an "active" unit with the maximum 40nm range. The "active" part is useful because it interrogates traffic outside of ground SSR coverage, but I think the 40nm range is of little value over somewhat cheaper boxes with 10-20nm range.

Like TCAS, the purpose of EGPWS (enhanced ground proximity warning system) under IFR is to prevent the remote chance of things going very badly wrong, so there is no real experience to report from 50 'normal' sectors. However, the record of CFIT accidents is such that I think terrain alerting is essential for this kind of transport IFR. The current certified GA version of EGPWS, "TAWS-B", has come down in price significantly in recent years, but is still relatively expensive. I think the non-certified terrain alerting system in the Garmin GNS430 (or MX20/GMX200) is very suitable for most light aircraft, and have also been impressed by a very professionally yoke-mounted Garmin 496 installation. I would not trust GPS topographic moving maps or various tablet PC and PDA gadgets as any kind of substitute.

5. En-route ATC across 15 countries

My enroute ATC experience was uniformly positive. The system is impressively seamless and well co-ordinated. There are only a few points worth noting:

Routes

There is a view amongst UK PPL/IRs that "you never fly the route you file". I think this must only apply to the busy airspace over central and southern England, because for the 40 sectors (80%) that were mainly outside the UK, I flew 20,000 route miles almost exactly as filed. The exceptions were direct-to clearances between filed route waypoints and the odd few minutes of radar vectoring for separation. In general, short cuts seem most likely if they are within a single FIR or ATC sector and in airways well away from the busy TMAs.

Communications

The phraseology across Europe is very standard. The UK has a slightly more formal and precise ATC style than most countries, which I think I prefer, although it does not make much practical difference. It's worth noting that "FL Wun Hundred" is unique to the UK, it's "FL Wun Zero Zero" elsewhere. Otherwise, you soon pick up the R/T nuances you didn't experience during IR training by listening to the airline and bizjet crews. I didn't find accented English was ever a barrier to understanding of ATC, nor was there very notable variation across different countries.

The five letter ICAO format for waypoint names is phonetic and distinct, but they are strange words that can be hard to comprehend over the radio. On a new route, it is worth studying all the waypoint names ahead of you, to avoid ATC having to spell out an unfamiliar one.

When changing frequencies on handover, I have learned to never fiddle with a prior frequency (e.g. to listen to ATIS) until you have successfully made contact with the next one.

En-route charts

I rarely glance at these in practice, but I would never be tempted to fly without published paper charts. A GPS nav-com, or an IFR chart on a laptop, is not a quick tool for locating an unfamiliar waypoint name or an ATC frequency. I have not found that enroute charts printed from JeppView are adequate; some items and legends are lost at different print scales in unpredictable ways.

6. GA IFR at major airports

Many of the 50 sectors were flown to main international airports, rather than the typical GA ones. This was sometimes my personal preference, but often it was necessary because the smaller alternative lacked some essential element of opening hours, IFR facilities, customs or ground services. In this section, I will try and detail the main differences I found operating in this environment, which may be unfamiliar to many PPL/IRs.

Pre-flight briefing

The Jepp section for a major airport can look daunting. Multiple runways, with a mix of CAT I and CAT II ILS and non-precision procedures, may result in a dozen different IAPs. Barcelona has 70 pages of departure procedures (DPs). Le Bourget arrivals involve an initial arrival chart, a continuation chart and then vectors from the end of the continuation to the start of the IAP. All of this complexity can be overcome with about 30mins of extra reading the first time you do the pre-flight planning to a new destination of this kind.

Firstly, you need to skim all the pages to get an overall sense of the content. If there are a large number of DPs and STARs, it's useful to work out how they are segmented (e.g. RNAV and non-RNAV, jet vs. prop) and linked to the different runways.

Secondly, you need to read the airport briefing pages and highlight the points relevant to you; especially on communications procedures and preferential runways. A lot of the material is about jet push-back, parking and noise abatement, but important points can hide in "jet-like" sections. You can then use your airways route, the 24hr TAF surface wind forecast and the preferred runway information to identify the most likely STAR and IAP, and mark them with post-it tabs. Be aware that, although your filed route will terminate at the start of a specific STAR, where there are several arrival procedures from the same general direction, ATC may choose to direct all traffic to a particular one, irrespective of filed routes.

Finally, you study the 10-9 airport chart and try and anticipate the taxiways to the GA apron; a specific designator can be hard to find on these charts and I carry A4 versions for big airports I am unfamiliar with.

Large airports can seem infested with obscure signage and markings, and it is worth revising the "ICAO recommended airport signs, runway and taxiway markings" pages near the end of the Jepp airway manual Introduction section. Taxiing amongst big jets is not stress-free, and you won't need the added stress of worrying about something like "is yellow on black taxiway location, and black on yellow taxiway direction, or vice-versa?". The same applies to the five colours used in surface lighting at night.

Descent and Arrival

Jet descent profiles are steeper than piston ones, so I usually ask for an early cruise descent and use 65% power and 500-700fpm as a way of gaining speed in the last 30mins of the flight and reducing block times a little. I have never had a problem with excessive ATC descent rate requirements, if I've sensibly anticipated the need for power reduction.

Approach and Landing

If there is jet traffic behind you, ATC may ask for 160KIAS to 4DME or the best speed you can manage. If there is a published minimum speed, you need to advise them if you can't make it. The 421C's gear and approach flap limits are 176KIAS, so this has not been an issue. Most piston aircraft have lower limits, and clearly ATC will not expect you to breach these or compromise safety. However, a major airport is not the place to be pedantic about 1.3x Vso and "gear down when intercepting the glide slope". Piston aircraft may have 3km more runway than they need, and I think one should plan and practice a non-conventional, but safe, high-speed approach technique for this kind of airport. You also should plan your touchdown to minimise runway occupancy time; avoid landing and then taxiing 500m to the nearest exit.

If conditions permit, accepting a visual approach will help ATC with spacing and may allow you to short-cut the IAP if other aircraft are not in the sequence ahead. You may, at times, want to have the option of arriving or departing VFR. At some airports, particularly in France, this will require VFR airport charts; you can download these from the national AIS/AIP site or buy the relatively inexpensive Bottlang product from Jeppesen.

Taxiing

Pre-briefing the airport chart, having a large paper copy to hand and being familiar with signage, markings and lighting are needed to make taxiing stress-free. At some airports, there are multiple handlers and multiple GA aprons; so when you first speak to ground control, it's useful to know your handler's stand designator, or where they intend parking you.

Operating at a large airport, I find myself aspiring to be as professional and competent as the airline crews around me, which I think this is a good thing up to a point. However, any kind of doubt, ambiguity or uncertainty during taxiing is a signal to stop safely and ask for help. Airports take surface movement safety and runway incursion very seriously, and a request for clarification, progressive taxi instructions or a follow-me van will invariably be met with a friendly and positive response. Professional crews regularly do this; not asking for assistance when unsure is the amateurish way.

A number of retrofit MFDs as well as the new glass panels offer GPS position-referenced airport charts. I use the Garmin MX20 with JeppView and find the taxiway charting very useful at a large and unfamiliar airport.

Slots

The departure time filed in a flight plan is the Estimated Off-block Time (EOBT) at which you intend to start taxiing. Busy airports use an airport slot system to manage the number of movements at peak times. Off-peak, slots may be unnecessary or very freely available. This slot is simply a 'local' airport permit to file a flight plan around a particular departure time. GA handlers will organise these, and advise you of any particular restriction or lack of capacity. Most airport slots seem fairly flexible.

The airways slot (sometimes called the ATC slot) is a Calculated Take-Off Time (CTOT), issued by Eurocontrol's Central Flow Management Unit (CFMU), in accordance with Air Traffic Flow Management (AFTM) policy, to impose a precise delay on a flight plan filed with CFMU's Integrated Initial Flight Plan Processing System (IFPS) when ATC capacity limits are predicted at any point along the filed route.

In practice, the slot system works as follows:

Case 1: At most airports and for most GA routes, we just file an FPL and it gets accepted by IFPS. We usually do this 1hr or more in advance, but often 15-30mins before EOBT is ok. We call ATC for start-up, get our clearance and depart.

Case 2: At some airports, we do exactly as in Case 1, but the EOBT has to be filed for a time we have been allocated as an airport slot. This is usually arranged well in advance, but the system is often flexible and ground handling services may be able to get a slot, or amend an existing one, at short notice.

Case 3: On some routes we do exactly as in Case 1 or Case 2, but, around 1hr before EOBT, we can get a message advising us that our departure is subject to an airways slot time, which is always precisely defined as a CTOT. This message will come from whoever filed the flight plan for us, or from ATC when we call for clearance delivery. When subject to an airways slot, the tower can not clear us to take-off more than 5mins before the CTOT or 10mins after it. We have to work back from this time, and plan start-up and taxiing accordingly. Some busy airports will specify the taxi times that must be assumed. The Homebriefing service (www.homebriefing.com) is an excellent way to file FPLs online, it has the advantage of sending airways slot messages and updates in real-time by email and SMS.

I apologise for not finding a simpler and more acronym-free way of explaining the slot system. Figure 3 illustrates that, in practice, airport and airways slots are usually a non-issue for even a fairly ambitious GA flight schedule, and they add little or nothing to the pre-flight planning workload.

Clearances and Start-up

At busier airports, you will often speak to a sequence of specialised ground frequencies (e.g. Clearance Delivery and Start-Up) before you start taxiing; the Jepp airport briefing plates explain these procedures. It's worth noting your stand number before getting in the aircraft, in case you can't see it from the cockpit.

Taxiing and Take-off

Once you call for taxi, you might be cleared directly to the hold and then for immediate take-off, with other aircraft waiting behind you. ATC are used to jets that don't stop to do run-ups, and have two crew to set up nav instruments and brief procedures. It's worth trying to get as much ready as possible before taxiing; you can ask to reposition on the apron for power and pre-take-off checks, and, if you haven't received your departure clearance, listen to the Ground frequency to identify and prepare the likely DP. Check the runway length available from any intersection takeoffs being offered. Note that a numbered holding point may be one of a set of line-abreast stands at a single large holding area.

Departure Procedures (DPs)

Most departures are straightforward, and often, on first contact with approach control, you will be cleared direct to the terminating point of the procedure and to your cruise level. However, single-pilot workload is high during the first few minutes of even a simple "turn to X, climb to Y" IFR departure. I find a more complicated DP (e.g. Figure 4) as difficult as any phase of IFR flight. It's worth planning these in detail, since we don't encounter the most complex ones often in the relatively terrain-free UK. Most of us fly IFR with GPS as the primary nav instrument and radio aids as a back-up. Unless you are confident you've mastered how the GPS will handle guidance and waypoint sequencing in all the obscure DP path-terminator combinations, you should forget the GPS, it will only confuse. Be aware that Jeppesen do not help, by sometimes using different waypoint designators in the GPS database from the airway manual plates.

Figure 4

LOJAS 1B	31	Climb on runway heading to GMM 3 DME, turn RIGHT, 133° heading, intercept 106° bearing from GM, when passing MGA R-155 turn LEFT to MGA, MGA R-026 to LOJAS.

There is a lot of terrain about in Europe, and, for piston aircraft, non-trivial DP gradients are also more common. These might require some adjustment to the usual cruise climb profile on a hot day, and planning engine-out scenarios in a twin.

Summary

Large airports can seem daunting and inaccessible. I hope this section is encouraging, despite listing a lot of differences from the typical GA IFR environment. A well-trained and current PPL/IR has done 99% of the work needed to operate safely at any large airport; it only needs some extra planning and a few operating practices that help you fit in with high-density commercial traffic.

7. Ground services

Ground handling

You generally have the choice of being handled by the airport operator or choosing a commercial handler, although at some larger airports the latter is the only option. Commercial handling costs between 50 and 200 euros for a piston aircraft, the airport operator is usually much cheaper. Every airport is different, so it is hard to generalise. Commercial handlers usually offer a consistently good service, and treat a small airplane pilot as courteously as their bizjet customers. Airport operator handling is somewhat variable. I personally use a commercial handler every time. Their job is to do whatever it takes to help you meet your schedule, and to make the transit comfortable. Planning is also much easier if you have an easily accessible, single point of contact. I find the cost and effort of GA too high to let the experience be spoiled by airport delays and hassles for the sake of a handling fee.

I carry a spare set of copies of just about every aircraft and pilot document an airport official might want, and have needed to hand these over a couple of times.

Refuelling

Avgas costs varied from 1 euro to 2.5 euros per litre across Europe during the period reviewed. Avgas supply, however, is the biggest single planning headache and cause of delay I have encountered. It is worth checking and rechecking availability if you are going to an airport that doesn't see much piston traffic. Paying for fuel will occasionally require either cash or the supplier's brand of fuel card. Credit cards are usually accepted, but the payment can take longer to process. I carry Shell, Exxon and BP cards, because it is fairly easy to get all three. Some suppliers will take another company's card, so it is worth asking. A Total card is useful in France, but you must have a French bank account. A Statoil card is useful in Scandinavia, and these are readily available.

However, the key lesson about fuelling is to always do so straight after you land. I have re-learned this lesson many times....

De-Icing on the ground

Aircraft seem to stubbornly retain surface ice even in bright sunshine and temperatures above freezing. From personal experience I can say that if your expectations of de-icing equipment are a handheld tank and sprayer, a large vehicle with a crane-mounted high-pressure hose is not a pleasant surprise, given the fluid costs several euros per litre. It can come to 500-1,000 euros for a small aircraft. The handheld tank variety is not available at many airports, so there is a strong incentive to carry your own.

8. Pre-flight planning

Some of the planning issues for this kind of flying have been discussed in the sections above, so I will only summarise the resources and process I use to try and make the task reasonably quick and easy. Most of these notes will be fairly obvious, but I'll detail them in case the reader finds some new and useful items. My 'system' takes two to four hours for a new destination, and 30-60 minutes to update the plan for a trip I've flown previously.

Website Resources

⌒ www.acukwik.com for airport data and contact details (fuel, handling).

⌒ www.avbrief.com for weather and NOTAMs; also has an excellent PDA/Blackberry/WAP interface.

⌒ www.cfmu.eurocontrol.int/chmi_public/ciahome.jsp?serv1=ifpuvs the IFPS flight plan validator.

⌒ www.homebriefing.com for filing FPLs.

⌒ www.interfax.net easy gateway service for faxing MS Office documents as email attachments.

⌒ www.pplir.org the *PPL/IR Europe* forum, has hundreds of members with specialised, local knowledge.

Software Resources

⌒ Jeppesen JeppView: for printing approach plates and reference to Jepp text pages.

⌒ Jeppesen FliteStar and internet WX subscription: for flight planning.

⌒ Jeppesen Services Update Manager: for updating GPS nav data and MX20 charts.

⌒ ICAO FPL form and UK GA Report (GAR): MS Word document *pro formas* with all my standard details filled in.

Hardware Resources

⌒ Home PC with a large Dell colour laser printer: for flight planning and printing trip kits.

⌒ Sony Vaio TX series laptop with Wi-Fi: for updating avionics data cards and flight planning whilst travelling.

⌒ Vodafone 3G USB data device: for laptop internet access when travelling.

⌒ Blackberry 8800: for weather data and mobile email (e.g. handling, FPL slots).

Other Resources

⌒ Various Jeppesen binders, Jeppesen paper for printing approach plates.

⌒ German DFS 24hr pay per call flight briefing and planning service +49 69 78072 550: as a back-up.

The only expensive, aviation dedicated items on this list are JeppView, which is essential, and the laser printer. I print hundreds of approach plate and flight plan pages every year and find an office-quality printer very useful – it's fast and will print double-sided colour plates on perforated Jepp binder paper.

Planning stage 1: Feasibility

As soon as I have a destination in mind, I try and work out whether flying myself is possible. I browse Jepp FliteStar to identify the likely destination and alternate airports, and run a quick flight plan to check the fuel burn and trip time. I then use the AC-U-KWIK website to get contact details of a commercial Ground handler. I call them and ask about avgas, opening hours, slots and any other restrictions. If all this is ok, I will email a handling request to get confirmation. I create a subfolder for the destination on my PC and save the handling contacts and a pdf of the AC-U-KWIK information page. This folder builds up to be the trip kit I print before travelling.

On some routes, I find it useful to research a second alternate. If your destination is the primary airport in a region, it may take two alternates to give you all the combinations of opening hours, IFR facilities and avgas supply you need. On longer range trips, it is also useful to identify an enroute fuel alternate.

Planning stage 2: Route

Getting IFPS-acceptable routes takes a little practice. First, I create a route using the FliteStar 'wizard' and amend it to start at a DP terminating waypoint and end at the initial waypoint of a STAR – this avoids a whole round of IFPS errors. I then paste the route into the Validator; about a third of the time it will come back with no errors, another third of routes will be ok after a tweak or two, and for the rest, I need to spend some time re-planning them, based on the error message feedback and the Route Availability Document on the CFMU site. I find routes along an axis between the southeast of England and northern Italy the most problematic, because the airways system is subject to a mass of availability restrictions, which FliteStar does not include in its database.

Once the route is accepted in the Validator, I create an FPL using my MS Word *pro forma* and save it in the trip folder. I also check the FliteStar route, enter the likely fuel, baggage and passenger load and save the route pack.

Planning stage 3: Night before

I get the airport NOTAMs for the departure, destination and alternate and print them for the trip kit. I also check and print the Sig WX and Spot Wind charts, and the 24hr TAFs.

I then update the FliteStar route pack with a download of the enroute winds. I've tweaked the aircraft performance model data so that I know it's accurate. I now have a detailed flight plan, JAR-OPS fuel plan and W&B schedule, which I save and print.

All the print-outs go into my trip kit: a small Jepp binder, with clear plastic page inserts. I maintain one large airway manual with all the plates for airports and alternates I use regularly. If the destination isn't one of these, I print the required plates. I also select the paper enroute charts needed. The trip kit is now complete, and it's all I take with me. I like not carrying a flight bag full of heavy manuals, and, if something changes, I have JeppView and FliteStar on my laptop as a back-up.

Finally, I file the flight plan with Homebriefing.com and use the email-fax gateway to send a GAR to Customs, Immigration and Special Branch as appropriate. Homebriefing lets you store FPL *pro formas*, so the aircraft and safety equipment fields don't need to be re-entered. I always save passenger GAR details, so I don't need to chase people for their passport numbers etc. the next time they travel.

Planning stage 4: Morning of flight
It's relaxing to wake up before the flight with no more planning to do or faxes to send; I only need to check the latest TAFs and airways slot messages, and then go to the aircraft. The IFPS route can be directly entered into the Garmin GNS480 units I use. A lack of FMS-style airways route handling is an irritating flaw in the Garmin 430 and 530 series. The 480s are coupled to an air data and fuel flow computer, so in flight, I only use the paper flight plan to note clearances and actual fuel burn and time enroute at key waypoints.

Planning stage 5: Return leg
The trip kit I take with me will have all the materials for the return journey except current weather. I will usually use a hotel Wi-Fi connection to download this and file the FPL. The FliteStar return leg print-out will be a zero-wind version, so I update this with forecast winds on the laptop and write in flight time and fuel burn changes by hand. The handlers will also give you a briefing folder with weather and NOTAMs for your route.

Regular destinations
When I have flown to a destination previously, things are a lot easier. A few days beforehand, I send the handling request, check airport NOTAMs and make sure the former route is still IFPS-valid. No more planning is needed until Stage 3, the night before.

Summary
This kind of 'real world' flight planning is never really taught in training or described in books or magazine articles. It takes some personal "R&D" time to develop methods that will work for you. However, although the IFR system looks very complex, it is also highly codified; once you "crack the code", it does become simpler.

PPL/IR Europe was founded because pilots like us are very much on our own; without the Ops departments and commercial service providers that support professional crews. The website, forum and journal are a very effective means of sharing knowledge and asking questions on all these flight planning topics. A request for help with a difficult IFPS route on the forum will usually get a reply in a few hours.

9. Safety conclusions
To what extent does this profile of self-flown transport IFR introduce new safety issues and how can they be managed?

Human factors and decision-making

Any transport flying, by definition, imposes some pressure to complete a flight. In planning a schedule, I think there are two ways to avoid over-stretching your aeronautical decision-making with difficult conflicts.

Firstly, the capability to execute flights safely must comfortably exceed the requirements of a travel schedule. I'll discuss some of the technical issues about capability in section 10, but the working day must also leave you fit to fly home. I find that 2-4hr flights between different cities are ok for a set of individual meetings, but not a series of long working days.

Secondly, the consequences of cancelling a flight must always be reasonably acceptable. On business, if a trip can be abandoned at short notice and easily rescheduled, that's fine. If it's a critical deal or meeting, then you must have a plan B. For personal travel, you have to be comfortable that the cost of private flying will occasionally include last-minute airline tickets, hotels and airplane recovery.

In practice, I find you naturally build these factors into the feasibility planning stage described above. Flying yourself is too much hassle if it's not going to be enjoyable and stress-free.

Standard operating procedures and single-pilot resource management

I think this profile of flying has several advantages. Firstly, you maintain relatively good IFR currency. Secondly, you gain good experience outside of comfortable, familiar routes. Thirdly, you operate in a highly controlled environment, scaled to airline safety needs; for example, I think it's easier to fly an ILS to minima at an airport with a 12,000 foot runway and full approach lighting than to a small regional airport.

However, each of these advantages brings a corresponding challenge, which I found needed adapting and firming-up my personal SOPs.

Complacency: My worst flying over this period didn't happen 1,000nm from home, during a complex procedure at an unfamiliar airport – it was always associated with getting complacent in undemanding conditions nearer to home. The effort to maintain SOP discipline needs to be greatest when you are most relaxed.

Sterile cockpit: I like having passengers who are interested in aviation, and some are fascinated by being in a light aircraft mixing with large jets. However, I have found that I need to be very blunt in briefing passengers that I can't speak to them at any time from brakes-off to cruise level and from top-of-descent to brakes-on.

Autopilot use: My procedure is to use the autopilot to fly the aircraft above 1,000 feet. I know some PPL/IRs are concerned about maintaining manual flying skills, and about autopilot failure. However, a high traffic density environment is not the place to practice single pilot hand-flying and it is not a place to fly (at least in a medium piston twin) without a reliable autopilot. The autopilot is the most basic safeguard against a momentary lapse which could result in an altitude bust or a loss of separation. For example, during multiple step climbs or descents, I think it is much more reliable to set the Alt Selector immediately after a clearance and monitor the autopilot capturing the assigned altitude than it is to hand-fly a level change. During IR training, the virtue of accurate hand-flying is so drummed into us, and rightly so, that I find I have to overcome a slight feeling I am being lazy or slack when I turn the autopilot on.

Operations manual

My original POH checklists do not include some key IFR operating procedures, and the autopilot and avionics checks are fragmented across various supplements at the back of the manual. I have written my own 20 page AOC-style ops manual for the aircraft, and I use a laminated, two-sided A4 extract as my checklist. I don't find after-market checklist products useful.

The PPL/IR website has an editable template of the SRM and single-pilot IFR operations manuals developed by our SRM working group, www.pplir.org/index. php?option=com_content&task=view&id=66.

10. Aircraft performance and equipment conclusions

This is a hard section to write, because aircraft owners are very loyal to their chosen types. Partly it's human nature, but also it's because the choice of aircraft and equipment is so inherently subject to individual mission needs, budgets and preferences. I know pilots who commute safely and reliably in a C172, and I know pilots who fret that their Citation CJ2 is too slow. I'll only comment on some specific aircraft features I developed a view on during the course of these 50 sectors.

Range

In practice, the requirement for a fuel stop is a very significant barrier to flying yourself on any kind of transport trip. Turnarounds that should be 45mins have a way of taking 90mins or more, and then your GA flight has used up much of the day to replace a 2hr airline flight. Long range is also very handy if it means that a round-trip can be flown without needing to worry about avgas cost or availability at the destination.

Speed

I think that where you live is the biggest factor determining what speed you require from a GA aircraft. If your home is three hours drive from Heathrow and 15mins from your local airport, almost any reasonable piston machine will be faster than airline travel for sectors within continental Europe. If you are based in the south of England, a 170KTAS airplane will get you to northern Spain, southern France or Switzerland in a realistic 3-3.5hrs. If you live in Glasgow, that becomes an unrealistic seven hours including fuel stop.

I find that a "practical radius" is 3-3.5hrs for weekend personal travel or a 24-48hr business trip.

Certified de-ice equipment

This is an interesting issue because I found the operational need for de-ice boots to be minimal, and yet without known-ice capability, I don't think I could have achieved anything approaching 98% flight completion. I love some of the new, technically advanced singles like the Cirrus and Columbia. However, any serviceable Seneca or

Aztec from the 1970s, fitted with $20k of modern avionics, is a vastly more capable transport machine. This is a problem for new designs, which are subject to more stringent icing certification and the critical performance of laminar-flow wings.

Pressurisation

Some pilots find portable oxygen a practical solution and some find that they and their passengers wouldn't contemplate the tubes, hoses and bottles involved. I found that flight above FL100 was required only in airways that crossed the Alps or Pyrenees, or to help get more direct routings through some TMAs. However, cruising above most weather in the quiet and comfort of a pressurised, air-conditioned cabin is very pleasant, and I think that some de-iced, pressurised piston types represent very good value in the used market.

Turbine engines

Avgas availability has been the single biggest planning problem and cause of delay during my transport flying. Even when airports and handlers assure you that avgas is available, you can turn up and find that there is none, or that it takes hours for the fuel supplier to attend to you. Madrid and Helsinki are two destinations I found that simply do not have an airport with both avgas and suitable IFR facilities and opening hours, and I suspect that the list will get longer over time. This makes the Diamond DA42 TwinStar a very attractive option for shorter range transport (e.g. up to 500nm) and used Piper Meridians or JetProp conversions ideal for one to three passengers on longer trips. Otherwise, the turbine entry level has a wide choice of $750k-$1.5m aircraft from the late 70s/early 80s 'golden age' of twin turboprops.

Summary

Because most GA piston airplanes are used for touring, training and hobby flying, I think the used aircraft market offers some quite good value for pilots with transport needs who are willing to ignore the conventional wisdom of hangar talk and pilot forums. The best value is in the unfashionable old light twins. You simply have to make an economic calculation that offsets higher fuel, maintenance and Eurocontrol charges against the cost of capital and depreciation in newer but less capable aircraft. De-iced Mooneys and Cessna 210s are good single-engine piston choices; but I think the Piper Malibu has the best combination of economics and performance. The 400-series Cessnas are viable as a low-cost alternative to an old King Air; the C340 is less expensive and has a smaller cabin. The Aerostar is the most compact but also the fastest pressurised piston twin.

The current market for new GA aircraft is somewhat polarised between the marginally capable piston sector and turbine aircraft costing $2m or more. However, the new single-engine personal jets being developed by Diamond, Cirrus and others may well change this significantly in future years. The 25,000 foot altitude, 1,000nm IFR range and 250-300KTAS performance of these types would be perfectly suited to the mission profile I've described.

11. Overall Conclusions

The cost of General Aviation is Europe is high, and its utility is limited by restrictions and regulations. However, a pilot can escape some of the PPR, hi-vis jacket, no-can-do misery inflicted on leisure pilots in the UK to find that Europe's IFR infrastructure is very effective and accessible. With an aircraft costing less than some luxury cars and an operating cost comparable to business class airline tickets, the determined PPL/IR pilot can benefit from the full flexibility and convenience of personal air travel. Achieving this safely and reliably does need maintenance, training, planning and operating standards which have many similarities to a commercial GA operator.

....by the way, did I remember to say "always refuel straight after landing"?

2 Flight planning away from base

By David Sowray

The first secret of successful flight planning away from base is to avoid it as much as possible. If it can't be avoided, the second secret is to be as self-sufficient as possible. Although most airfields around Europe provide just-adequate flight planning facilities for pilots, there are a few problems which crop up on a regular basis:

- The facilities are frequently spread out around the airfield, with the weather in one place, the flight plan filing in another and the landing fee payments at a third.

- It is not unusual for systems not to be working, or for it to be unclear how they work with nobody around to help. Language difficulties also compound this problem. Some systems need passwords or registration.

- Although systems are provided for weather and filing flight plans, I have never seen anything to help with what is usually the thorniest problem - working out what route to file. That said, often the operations staff know the best routes into and out of their own airport, but once you are beyond their local area, you are on your own.

These problems may not individually be insurmountable, but they can add up to make a journey far more stressful than it needs be. As a rule, the problems are much less significant for airfields and routes with which you are familiar so they tend not to crop up much in training. But once straying into unknown territories the problems start to be encountered more frequently and obstacles which on their own are small tend to compound. In my experience, for serious travelling to unfamiliar destinations around Europe, the ability to be as self-sufficient as possible makes life much easier.

In part, these problems are related to the dispatch reliability you need and the flexibility you have in timings. It is possible, for example, to file an unchecked route on your flight plan and experiments by **PPL/IR Europe** members have shown there is a good chance the route will either be perfectly acceptable or will come back accepted with small corrections. However, there are occasions when it does not and when that happens, you can find yourself depending on the kindness of strangers. Solving whatever glitch has occurred can then be an open-ended problem, with possible knock-on effects and the potential to delay flights timed later in the day beyond the closing time of airports.

In discussing the possible technology solutions, I have tried as much as possible to steer away from specific recommendations. Firstly, such information tends to go out of date very quickly. Secondly, there are so many different combinations of equipment that it's impossible to cover all the options in this short article. Thirdly, there are many trade-offs involved in choosing the best solution and it is very much a matter of personal preference in putting together the best solution for each individual.

Planning a route away from base

One of the most difficult tasks away from base is replanning a route from scratch. This can happen if plans change or if, for example, you wish to take a different route to avoid an area of bad forecast weather. Although it's possible to work out a theoretical route using just the Jeppesen or Aerad airways charts, it needs a computer and an internet connection to use the flight plan checker on the CFMU website. The changed route may also need new plates, which for European touring generally means printing either from JeppView or from the various European AIS internet sites.

The computer can be pretty much any laptop able to connect to the internet and to run JeppView, if you have it. With the increasing availability of Wi-Fi connections in hotels and airports around the world, fast internet connectivity is becoming less problematic. It is not uncommon to find unprotected wireless access in many pilots' lounges specifically provided for the purpose of flight planning. If Wi-Fi access isn't available, a GPRS connection can be used, usually in conjunction with a mobile phone connected to the laptop using infra red, Bluetooth or a cable.

The ability to print is very useful, indeed almost essential for approach plates, but adds yet more to the complexity of what's required. Reasonably portable printing solutions do exist, such as the Canon iP90 and the beautifully small but horribly expensive Pentax PocketJet, but they are yet one more thing to carry, maintain and keep supplies for. Indeed, although I myself have a Canon iP90, I do not find it worth carrying with me on trips and prefer to rely on ad hoc solutions.

The easiest ad hoc solution I've found, which I picked up from another *PPL/IR Europe* member, was to download the free CutePDF printer drivers and use these to "print" whatever you need to pdf files. These pdfs can then be transferred to a memory stick and passed to the hotel reception who generally seem quite amenable to printing them on paper for you. An alternative to this approach is to e-mail the pdfs to a GMail or Hotmail account and then use the hotel's internet service or a local internet cafe to print them out. If neither of these two solutions work, in desperation it may also be possible to fax them to yourself at the hotel, although I guess this is likely to be the most expensive way of doing it.

Incidentally, the worst solution I've so far found for approach plates is to use a tablet PC to display them directly in the cockpit. Although I had previously considered this a viable option in a squeeze, having tried it once I would now be very reticent to rely on it again in all but the most benign weather. It is only once you try to use it that you realise how dependant you have suddenly become on something which has so many different ways to fail.

Choosing your laptop

The choice of laptop or tablet computer best suited to the itinerant pilot is far too big a topic to be covered here. Much information on the topic can be gleaned from the internet. Amongst the many useful articles *PPL/IR Europe* member Peter Holy has written is a summary of his experiences setting up a Motion LS800 tablet computer to use in his aircraft, which can be found at: www.peter2000.co.uk/ls800/index.html.

In summary, the main points to consider are:

- The laptop size, weight, screen resolution and form. Obviously the smaller and lighter it is, the easier to carry around. However the smaller machines tend to have lower resolution screens which display less information. If it is a tablet PC it's less cumbersome in the cockpit, but without a keyboard, data entry can be slower. There are some PCs, such as the Fujitsu Lifebooks, which convert from one input method to another. It is worth bearing in mind that whatever the native resolution, for home use it's usually possible to plug in a full-size high resolution screen and a separate keyboard and mouse.

- The connection options are important to consider, so that you can attach to the internet via Wi-Fi or a mobile phone acting as a modem. For the latter, it is worth considering a laptop with Bluetooth and an infrared port. Direct connections via USB cables are often possible, but inevitably the cable will be sitting at home when you most need it.

- Screen brightness can be an issue when trying to use the PC in an aircraft. Some are substantially easier to read than others in direct sunlight.

- Battery life is obviously important. In addition, the ability to plug the PC into accessory sockets to run off aircraft power can be worth having. Although this is usually possible, it is not a common requirement and as a result the power cords can be stupidly expensive. Be careful, also, of compatibility between the output voltage of the accessory socket and the input voltage the computer power supply requires.

⌒ As hard disks are generally limited to being used at altitudes of 10,000 feet or less, for in-flight use it may be worth considering installing a solid-state hard drive.

With the rapid changes in technology, no doubt in years to come there will be better options emerging. Recently people have been looking at products like the Sony Reader for displaying approach plates in-flight. There are also some similar products specifically designed for the aviation market, often intended primarily for the US market, although none of these appears to have solved all the problems involved adequately yet.

Pre-flight weather, NOTAMS and flight plan filing

With the exception of planning a totally new route and printing approach plates, SIDs and STARs, most other pre-flight planning tasks can be achieved using a mobile phone with a built-in internet browser. If you already have your small laptop suitable for flight planning available, it is much easier to also use that for all the remaining flight planning tasks. However, this is not always practical, especially for shorter, one-day trips, or those where you're out and about, or if you already have a lot of baggage to carry to your hotel.

Having myself started using a truly mobile solution a number of years ago for getting weather via the internet and filing flight plans (in my case using a Nokia 9210 to fax them through to the Heathrow Flight Plans Unit) I now find it essential to have something genuinely portable. The flexibility it brings you is very valuable. It allows you to leave your flight plan filing until you are already on your way or just about to leave for the airport and can estimate your EOBT accurately. It is especially valuable when travelling with passengers who inevitably add a certain amount of unpredictability and never appreciate being dragged away early or hanging around airports waiting for the EOBT to arrive.

Although it is often nice to have paper print outs, for example of weather or your flight plan, it is generally not vital. TAFs and METARs can be noted down by hand, and graphical data, such as the Met Office model charts, can often be saved locally to the phone for later browsing.

It is important, though, to try using all of the websites you will need before you actually do need them. Some appear at first sight to work fine, but are not usable in practice. Others have got small "gotchas", which need work-arounds. One of the most common is for complex menus and links not to work properly on the mobile device. This problem can be circumvented by storing a bookmark to the specific page you need rather than going through the menu page, but you need to know what that page URL address is before you can use it.

Some websites are much more mobile-device friendly, having been designed with them in mind and it is worth finding out beforehand which these are.

Mobile device choice

Often, the choice of mobile device to use is fixed. For many people the choice of mobile phone is driven by other everyday considerations, rather than being bought specifically to meet aviation needs. They are often provided by employers, or perhaps need to support Blackberry e-mail or other specific applications or operating system. It is impossible to go into detail about the huge range of mobile phones currently available, and the information would soon go out of date; but as a broad overview as of the end of 2007, there are a number of common types of SmartPhone operating system, amongst the most prevalent of which are:

- Windows mobile, used in a number of SmartPhones from a range of manufacturers. This operating system is often also found in some PDAs, such as the HP iPAQ range.

- Symbian OS, used in many Nokia, Samsung and Sony phones.

- Blackberry phones, which use a manufacturer-specific operating system.

- Some manufacturer-specific operating systems, such as found in Apple iPhones

- Nokia Communicators - the 9500 and 9300 models, which use an older version of the Symbian operating system. Although somewhat obsolete, these are still available and deserve a special mention only because they are probably the last phones to support fax sending and receiving without having to subscribe to an e-mail to fax service.

The main difference between each operating system type is their ability to access the different flight-planning related websites. One of the most useful, but most difficult, is Austro Control's excellent Homebriefing website, which allows you to file and change flight plans. For pilots on the move, this is an incredibly useful facility. Unfortunately, the browser which comes with version 5 of the Windows Mobile operating system does not work with the Homebriefing website. Annoyingly, it appears to work fine right up until you press the button to submit the flight plan, at which point nothing happens.

One current unknown is whether the rumoured web-based flight plan submission system for the UK will be usable from any mobile phones. This may become more of an issue as Homebriefing introduce charges for flight plans which do not either start or end in their own region. Fortunately, Homebriefing's charges do not appear prohibitive, given how useful and generally efficient the service is.

The Symbian-based mobile phones, conversely, appear to work satisfactorily with Homebriefing as well as many other flight planning websites.

If choosing a mobile phone specifically for aviation use, in addition to being able to access the websites you require, the most important features to look out for are:

⌒ A proper keyboard. Obviously, predictive text is not much use when entering flight plan details or ICAO identifiers and it quickly becomes frustrating trying to do it with the number keys found on most mobile phones.

⌒ A larger size screen is very useful. Again, the Homebriefing site is a good test, as the flight plan input form is designed for viewing on a desktop display. Many screens are similar sizes, with the Nokia N91, the Blackberry 8300 and many of the Windows Mobile devices such as the Motorola Q9 having a display resolution of 320x240. By comparison, the Apple iPhone is 320x480 pixels. Current king of the castle is the new Nokia E90 Communicator which comes with an 800x352 screen, but does not have the built-in fax facility of the older Nokia Communicators.

⌒ An increasingly common and very useful facility is the ability to connect to wireless networks. Although this does not give you any more functionality than connecting through your network's GPRS service, when abroad it is often very much cheaper.

⌒ In order to use the phone as a GPRS modem for your computer, you need a way of connecting the two together. If your laptop computer also has Bluetooth, this is the most convenient option and quite common nowadays. If not, either an infrared port or connecting through a cable are second choices.

One of the most useful facilities to have remains the ability to send faxes. This can be done from most mobile phones using one of the many e-mail to fax services. It can also be useful to be able to receive faxes via these services. The e-mail to fax services most commonly recommended by **PPL/IR Europe** members has been InterFax - www. interfax.net - which just requires prior registration and the payment of a minimum £10 credit.

Although arcane, faxes can still be used both to file flight plans and for customs requests. When faxing official forms, such as the CA48 flight plan, it is generally easier to send them using a PC or the traditional paper and fax machine combination. However it is rare that a free-text alternative is not also perfectly acceptable as, for example, I've always found with filing flight plans. Although the format of the flight plan text appears a little complicated at first, it is very easily mastered. The CFMU flight plan assistant outputs the input fields in free text format, providing a simple way to translate a flight plan. Having done it once, it is very easy then to edit old flight plans rather than having to re-enter them from scratch.

The most important step to take if you are planning to rely on any equipment, service or website for pre-flight planning away from base is to test it out properly before you actually need to use it. There are frequently small glitches which could easily be circumvented with forethought. It is much easier to do this beforehand, rather than when under time pressure of an impending departure.

Useful websites for pre-flight planning

Below is a brief description of some of the most useful websites for flight planning away from base; this is not intended to be an exhaustive list, just a selection of what is available. Inevitably, as time goes on some of these will disappear or change and some new ones will appear.

Many of the sites require registration prior to use, and in some cases payment of a subscription.

www.homebriefing.com

As already mentioned, the Homebriefing website is one of the few which allows any pilot to file a flight plan departing and landing anywhere. IFR flight plans appear to get routed automatically into the Eurocontrol IFPS and confirmations of acceptance (and notification of any slots) are usually received by e-mail or SMS within mere minutes of entering them into the website. For pan-European touring, many pilots find it an incredibly useful tool which saves messing about trying to find local fax numbers and working fax machines.

Whilst there are plans to start charging for flight plans which do not start or finish in either Austria or Switzerland, the proposed charges do not appear unreasonably high. A similar Dutch system also currently provides a similar service, but this will soon be restricted to local pilots or flights.

Homebriefing generally appears reliable while in comparison, of the four times I have used Olivia (a French flight planning site http://olivia.aviation-civile.gouv.fr), on two occasions ATC at the departure airport had no record of the flight plan.

The Homebriefing site does also provide pre-flight weather and NOTAM briefing services. These work fine, but they are not particularly well implemented and have nothing special to recommend them.

As mentioned earlier, however, the site is impossible to use with a Windows Mobile browser as the flight plan "Send" button simply does not work. It appears to work satisfactorily with the Opera browser and users of the Nokia E61 style phones report it works well with those too.

www.avbrief.com

Although Avbrief also provide NOTAMs, this is primarily a weather site. Along with the Met Office, they are one of the few officially sanctioned sources of pre-flight weather information. From a mobile user's point of view, the website is slightly cheaper to use as there is less overhead downloading unnecessary, fancy graphics and menu systems. However, it is not the simplest site to use from a mobile, with slightly unclear links to many of the graphical products.

Some support is also provided specifically for mobile users with a WAP site at www. avbrief.co.uk/wap.wml which provides access to current TAFs and METARs.

yaws.mobi

This is a free website provided by www.activitae.com and is one of the few specifically intended to be used from a mobile phone. It has been cleverly designed to be accessible from a wide range of phones, supporting simple WAP browser phones in addition to the more sophisticated Smartphone's with built-in internet browsers.

The acronym "YAWS" stands for Yet Another Weather Service, which gives a good hint of what the website provides. In addition to the textual weather products, such as TAFs and METARs, the more sophisticated phones can access graphical products such as the Met Office 214/5 forms and synoptic charts.

pda.meteox.com

This site is very useful for those without on-board weather radar, as it provides access to slightly delayed weather radar for much of Europe. The PDA site can be very useful for a last-glance check before take-off. Indeed, I have used it like that myself in deciding whether to route west or east of London on a return trip from northern France with a band of active weather crossing the region. However one matter to be careful of is that they do not receive radar feeds for some areas which are represented on the display map. These could then appear to be totally clear of rainfall even when there is activity.

www.ais.org.uk

The NATS pre-flight briefing site is one of those that needs prior planning if you intend to use it from a mobile phone. Although this is possible, it is not easy.

The first problem some find is that clicking the blue tick mark on the logon page with a mouse pointer does not work on some mobiles. I have so far found "tabbing" the highlighted field down to the tick mark and hitting the enter key works on every mobile I have tried so far.

Once the main page comes up, a more difficult problem arises, as the menu system used to access the website functions either does not appear, for example on Windows Mobile browsers, or is practically impossible to use, for example on the Nokia 9500 Opera browser. The best way of circumventing this problem is to save bookmarks to the specific pages you will want to access. For example, to get a NOTAM Narrow Route Briefing, create a bookmark to: www.ais.org.uk/aes/control/ww_briefing?HF_ACTION=newnarrow.

In conclusion

If you can arrange access to these websites, most of your immediate pre-flight planning needs will be catered for.

Of course, none of this is compulsory and others have shown that you can successfully fly quite extensive European tours just relying on the facilities and local knowledge at each airport en-route. Whilst some of them are indeed very well kitted out with informed and helpful staff, my own experience is that increasingly nowadays you arrive at a briefing room to find it empty apart from a single terminal. If you're lucky it is working and there is a queue to use it. If you are not, it is broken and there is nobody around to point you in the direction of an alternative. This may be fine sometimes, but inevitably it will happen when you are under most pressure to depart on time, for example when you need to reach your destination airport before it closes, or when you have got three grumpy passengers in tow wanting to get home.

If you are trying to use the aircraft as an efficient transport tool, whether for business or pleasure, only a relatively small investment is needed to make yourself totally self-sufficient. Mostly the equipment just makes gathering pre-flight information more slick and less hassle, but on rare occasions I have found mine really vital. Having been saved the expense and inconvenience of at least one unscheduled overnight stop, I have found the investment of time and money to get it right well worth making.

3 Preparing and maintaining your aircraft for IFR flying

By Jim Thorpe

The old adage about flying over water is that the engine does not know where it is. That may be true but firstly the pilot does and secondly if there is an engine problem the chances of a good outcome are severely reduced. The same applies to flying in IMC and at night. There are three main issues. An engine failure in a single-engine aircraft will mean a forced landing with restricted, perhaps minimal, opportunity to select an emergency landing site. Less obvious are a whole range of failures which while unwelcome in VMC will be significantly more difficult to handle in IMC. Of course we practice some rather arbitrary partial panel exercises from time to time but this is only one of a whole range of events which can ruin your day if you allow yourself to be distracted from the prime task of flying the aircraft. Thirdly if IFR you tend to be high, certainly FL90 perhaps FL200 or higher. If the engine fails this gives you more time to take remedial action and is a 'good thing'. If you are on fire it is not a 'good thing'. Speaking as one who discovered fuel dripping on my leg at FL90 in sold IMC over the Czech republic, the emergency descent taking vectors to an unknown airfield (pre GPS days) seemed to take a very long time.

Let's turn to some specifics.

Vacuum pumps

The attitude indicator is your key instrument and it is usually powered by the vacuum system. Vacuum pumps fail. Mortality is much increased in the first 20 hours and from say 400 hours onwards. Change pumps automatically at about 500 hours and try to avoid hard IMC for a few hours after the change. Don't adopt the false economy of failing to change the hoses and the filters at the same time. Most vacuum pumps rely on carbon vanes as seals. They do not need oil lubrication (hence they are known as dry pumps) but they will be trashed by a small amount of dirt or oil. If you fly serious IFR and you think the turn coordinator is adequate back up you are playing Russian roulette and the only argument is how many empty chambers before the bullet. You can have an electric AH, a standby electric vac pump or one of the fall back systems which work off manifold pressure. If you are a belt and braces person you can get electric AH with its own battery back up. Really flying serious IFR without a second AH with a different power source is leaving your safety pretty much to chance.

Regular maintenance

Always have a 50 hour/six month check. Don't do it yourself even if its legal. Having a highly experienced engineer look over your aircraft even while doing mundane things like oil changing may result in spotting faults you yourself would never notice. On one occasion my engineer spotted a nut within two threads of a parting company with its bolt which would have left me without a throttle linkage. He was at the time engaged on an entirely unrelated trivial task. This kind of aptitude is only acquired with thousands of hours of experience leading to a sense for things that are not quite right.

If you are at all mechanical try to improve your own knowledge. Clean the aircraft and the engine from time to time. Try to look it over in a purposeful manner. Learn what an exhaust leak stain looks like. Very small exhaust leaks especially on a turbocharged engine can be very dangerous. Look for marks that indicate something is rubbing where this should not be the case. Try over time to build up your own feeling for what isn't quite right but recognise that you will always fall well short of the abilities of someone who spends their whole working life looking at engines.

Train your engineer

Having said how valuable a trained eye is your engineer will almost certainly have been influenced by his average customer who is probably focussed on cost rather than value. Let your engineer know that you do fly in difficult conditions and that while you don't have bottomless pockets, you do want him to exercise some thoughtful additional care and involve you in any risk verses cost decisions. Some specific issues will be covered later.

Don't waste too much time on worrying whether Service Bulletins are compulsory or not. There are a few SB's which are motivated by manufacturer's liability concerns and are of little practical use. However the vast majority reflect real-world experience of real problems. Talk to your engineer. Understand the issues. Where appropriate have him do the work and pay the bill.

A proper oil change

Change your oil every 50 hours or six months irrespective of use. It is the best thing you can do to save money in the long run. When you change the oil take a sample (full flow and in a new plastic bottle don't contaminate the sample) and send it for analysis. Establish trends. Oil analysis is generally useless on a one-off basis but do it at every change and the record of variations can give early indications of trouble. Get your engineer to cut the oil filter not just change it. Tell him you want it done with the correct tool (hacking it apart just creates metal particles which confuse the issue) and that you want the pleats of material that filter the oil washed and the residue kept for you to see. Tell him you understand this is a messy unpopular job but you want it done properly. If there are any particles at all (even if the engineer says this is normal) preserve them in a plastic bag for future comparison.

Engine analyser

An engine analyser which tells you the EGT and CHT of every cylinder is a great safety feature on any engine. If you have a larger engine especially if it is turbocharged this equipment is almost mandatory. It will pay for itself in fuel savings and used intelligently will extend the life of your engine. Get one that records the data, download the record regularly and keep it on file. You will either have to work at understanding what the data can tell you or obtain the help of someone knowledgeable. Having a record of the EGT and CHT of every cylinder every few seconds will give you early indications of a whole range of potentially dangerous problems. It might also give you advance warning of something which can be fixed very cheaply now but which will be very expensive if not dealt with till the nasty noises become audible.

Climbing out of Gloucester on an IFR clearance I could make no sense of the readings on my Engine Analyzer. The aircraft was climbing well, there were no unusual indications on any other instrument and no strange noises. I persuaded myself it was some electrical gremlin but on reaching FL 90 just before the airway join I heard a tiny 'ping'. A flood of belated common sense lead to a pan call and a priority return. During the long descent for the NDB/DME approach there were just a few more barely audible 'pings' to make me wonder if I was over reacting. On the ground it only took a glance under the cowling to see that one cylinder had cracked severely and the escaping gasses were torching the adjacent cylinder to the extent that its fins were burning off and hitting the cowling with a just audible 'ping'. The engine analyser was trying its best to tell me I was in trouble. I didn't need to identify the problem in flight although with hindsight that would have been possible. I just needed to know that the indications were not normal and action was needed.

The INOP sticker

There are truths in aircraft operation that defy logic. If you drop a pencil it will slide immediately to the most inconvenient and inaccessible portion in the cockpit. Rather more seriously so will a dropped approach chart. In a similar way stickers placed on equipment to indicate that it is inoperative seem to breed. You rarely see one on its own and that is a certain indication of an ownership approach that does not bode well for IFR flying. Most aircraft equipment is there for a purpose and if it is genuinely redundant then it should be permanently removed. Perhaps worse is the equipment that is not exactly 'inop' but rather works if you don't need it. The ADF that comes alive at ten miles from the beacon, the DI that precesses to the extent that resetting it becomes a distraction. It may be possible to accept this sort of thing for VFR flying and still retain an acceptable safety margin but it is unacceptable in an aircraft expected to fly IFR.

Cockpit management

The theme running through this chapter is that in IMC the margins for error are reduced. It becomes important that you can find what you need without delay. Most light aircraft have less than adequate stowage within reach of the pilot so make the best use of what there is. Relegate the items that you don't need in flight like fuel drains or the screwdriver that opens the cowling to stowage that is of little or no use in flight. (Give a thought to dual purpose items such as fuel drains needed to operate the emergency gear lowering as in some twins). In US aircraft it is a legal requirement for the flight manual to be within reach in flight. Certainly the basics of pencils, charts, checklists, plates, glasses and sick bags should occupy consistent known locations so they are readily available if needed in a hurry.

Back up

The day the aircraft's electrical system dies you will be very glad of a portable GPS and a hand held radio. You will be less pleased when you find that the handheld's performance is very poor indeed unless you have an external aerial and connectors to enable it to operate with your headset. The latest portable GPS are extremely capable and have good battery life. The day you need it immediately is not the time to discover that you have not changed the batteries or recharged the battery pack for years. A small sticker noting the date the equipment was last charged or batteries changed can address this and of course this applies to the hand held radio as well. In an ideal world you will also have spare battery pack within reach and you will know how to perform the sometimes fiddly task of effecting the change. In benign conditions you can hold the GPS but in hard IMC this is less likely to be acceptable. Give some thought to how you would locate the GPS in a moment of crisis. The weighted mats supplied with some units for use in cars can work well depending on your cockpit layout. If you can develop a means of keeping the unit within your line of sight you might like to experiment with using it as an emergency aid for limited panel flying. You must make your own decision in the light of practical experience but I find it far easier to use a portable GPS for limited panel flight than to use the turn co-ordinator in the traditional manner.

In more complicated aircraft it is worth turning off the electrics on a VFR day to see what doesn't work. I was surprised to discover in a real failure situation that engine management became an issue. Fortunately it was VMC with another pilot on board but we were over hostile terrain a long way from any diversion so fuel needed to be conserved as did battery power to ensure gear lowering and ATC liaison at the destination. As I operate my aircraft lean of peak I am reliant on engine instrumentation to monitor

EGT (exhaust gas temperature) and TIT (turbine inlet temperature). This meant that when all the engine instruments read zero it was unwise to make any throttle, mixture or RPM changes in a situation where it was also unwise to simply operate the engine full rich for cooling.

Long distance trips

One of the advantages of the IR is the ability to fly to more distant destinations. This may expose you to situations where maintenance support is hard to come by and you can suffer considerable inconvenience with failures that would be relatively trivial within reach of your home base. Of course it's just not possible to cover every eventuality but, depending on the type of aircraft, your own capabilities and the potential downsides it is possible to take steps. If your aircraft type is very common spares are more likely to be available and, assuming you know the sources, Fedex can get them almost anywhere in the world within a day or so. If your model is rare and you know that spares are an issue you might choose to hold spares at home or even carry them with you if weight allows. If you are lucky enough to find a local engineer he may not have key aircraft specific data. It is now possible to get the maintenance and spares manuals on CD at reasonable cost so these can always be carried. If you feel able to perform some maintenance tasks you will need appropriate tools. For example if you are flying in the less developed parts of the world a spare tyre and the tools and ability to change it can mean the difference between a couple of hours delay and sleeping in the aircraft for several days to ensure that it is not dismantled and sold in your absence.

  If you are reasonably confident that you will be keeping your aircraft for some time holding some key spares can avoid delay and frustration during regular maintenance. Sometimes it can even save money as the cost of aircraft parts 'needed yesterday' can sometimes be very different to a part sourced without any time pressure. Please don't think that because you used to mess with cars you will somehow manage with the aircraft. Get involved with your aircraft engineer in advance and work with him on the tasks which you think fall within your abilities. Recognise that you will slow him down and he certainly won't charge less for any work performed in this way. Please remember that these thoughts relate to dealing with emergency situations. It may or may not be legal to perform the task so you will need to check out specific situations with your own engineer. For my somewhat unusual aircraft I stock a starter, a magneto, governor, spark plugs, nose wheel and main wheel tyres and tubes and an oil filter.

Conclusion

I can understand a pilot feeling that all this is a bit too much trouble but I suggest that he would be wrong. Depending on the complexity of the aircraft and the type of flying a lot more could be said. Some pilots consider a single transponder unacceptable as its failure will prevent entry to the IFR system. Some aircraft have de ice and oxygen systems which come with their own set of advantages and potential problems. The list goes on. I suggest that putting some thought into what you want out of your flying, predicting potential problems and developing strategies to help resolve them will always lead to more enjoyable, relaxed and satisfying flying. On rare occasions this forethought will make a real contribution to a safe outcome from some incident.

4 Icing tactics

By Robert Lough

This is an updated version of an article that first appeared in Instrument Pilot Issue 48 (March-April 2005), and was edited by Ole Henriksen. The author holds a JAA CPL/MEL/ IR and has been flying a Piper Aztec in Europe since 2000. The article focuses on practical planning for flying in potential structural icing conditions in low level airways using piston equipment - it does not address carburettor icing.

The author flies 80-100 hours a year, mainly on airways, between the UK, Eire and within Continental Europe. Typically, between September and May, around half the cross country flights have the potential to be exposed to some icing conditions. This is either due to climbing or descending through clouds that have the potential to produce ice, or freezing fog conditions at departure or destination. Given the typical MEA of low level airways in Europe of around FL70 through FL110 (outside mountainous regions), there is a practical risk of icing in climb/descent in the winter. In the cruise, icing conditions can be encountered at these levels also in spring and autumn. Flying over mountainous terrain has the potential for icing encounters year -round, and a conservative, but realistic, assessment would hold that non-turbine GA equipment, even with de-icing, is marginal in coping with ice over mountains.

1970's light twins and emergence of TKS

The Piper Aztec, with the proper equipment, is certified to fly into known icing conditions FIKI (light to moderate icing), with the de-icing equipment in good operating condition. The anti-icing and de-icing equipment on an Aztec consists of: cabin windscreen defroster, pitot heat, alternate air selection for both engines, pneumatic boots driven by dual vacuum pumps on wing, stabilator and rudder leading edges, electrically heated de-ice pads on the propellers (driven by dual alternators), and electrically heated windscreen de-ice plate on the pilot's side. This is supplemented by an ampere meter to check functioning of the propeller de-ice pads, and an ice light to monitor proper functioning of the boots. The Aztec has a wing based on the Piper Cub airfoil with a relatively thick cross section and a well rounded leading edge. As icing forms more easily on small radius airfoils, the thick Cub-like airfoil of the Aztec provides some advantage in an icing encounter. The excess power of twin engines also provides some extra margin for dealing with icing encounters.

The Piper Aztec, Piper Seneca and Cessna 310 were produced in reasonable numbers with FIKI certification (in the case of the Beech Baron, while having optional de-icing equipment, only a smaller proportion of models actually gained FIKI certification). Until recently these 1960/1970 twin piston aircraft represented the bulk of the FIKI GA fleet, however new generation aircraft with FIKI certification are today becoming the norm (see below).

In the 1990s TKS weeping wing technology started to be delivered commercially to GA, and today, through an STC, a relatively long list of aircraft can gain FIKI certification either at manufacture, or as an after-market item, e.g.: BE36, Mooney, Baron, Twin Star. The TKS system has glycol pumped through laser-drilled titanium panels on the leading edge of the wings and elevator/stabilator, in addition to a slinger wheel for the prop(s), and an application bar for the windscreen. The system requires redundancy in the pumps, and adequate reserves of de-icing fluid. It also extracts some payload penalty as an adequate reservoir contains around 40-60 lbs of fluid.

Operating a GA aircraft with suitable de-icing equipment in the Northern Europe airways environment requires a conservative set of operating limitations to remain both legal and maintain acceptable safety standards. If the aircraft has no de-icing equipment (other than pitot heat), the operating limitations are stricter.

What do the databases say?

In updating the article the author used both the NTSB database and the AOPA ASF (Air Safety Foundation) database.

In the case of the NTSB, a limited sample of typical GA aircraft used in IFR conditions (Beech 36 and 58, Cessna 210, 310, and 421, Mooney, Piper Piper PA23, PA30, PA32, PA34 and PA46) were sampled for the period 1994 through 2007. This produced 74 accidents during the 14 year period, with the majority of the accidents (55%) involving fatalities.

Chart 1 below shows the distribution of accidents by type, split between single-engine and multi-engine. It would appear that there is a higher accident rate amongst twins given they represent a smaller portion of the overall fleet, and yet in this period the

Chart 1: Aircraft Total Accidents

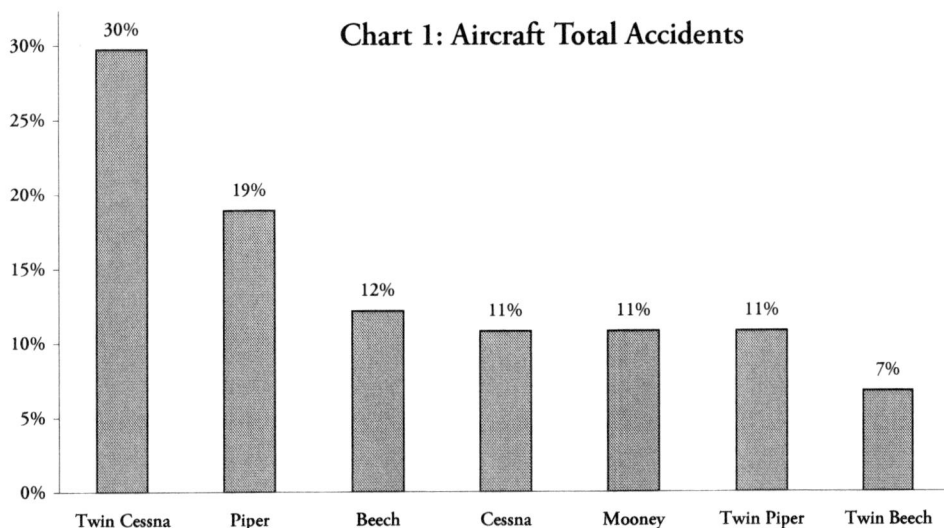

Twin Cessna	30%
Piper	19%
Beech	12%
Cessna	11%
Mooney	11%
Twin Piper	11%
Twin Beech	7%

Chart 2: Aircraft Fatal Accidents

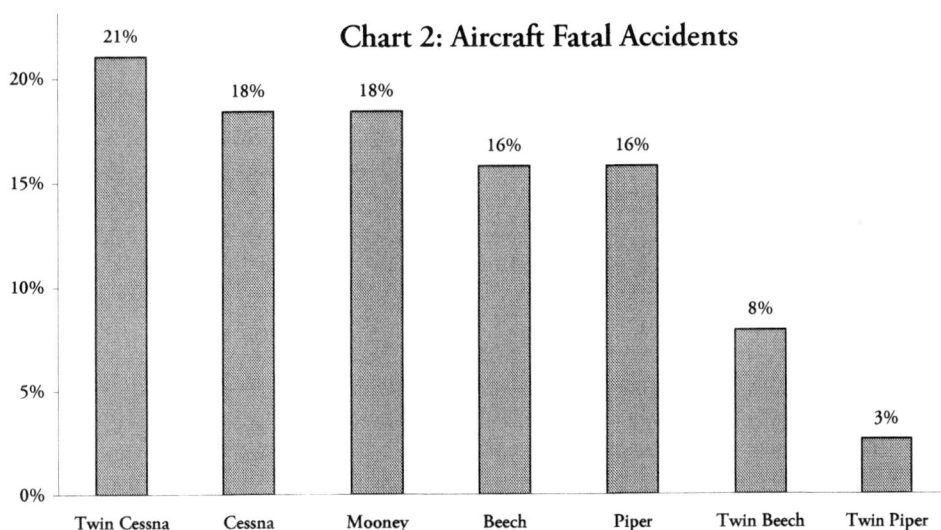

Twin Cessna	21%
Cessna	18%
Mooney	18%
Beech	16%
Piper	16%
Twin Beech	8%
Twin Piper	3%

twins accounted for 47% of the accidents where structural icing was a possible factor. This reflects that the twins may be used more in earnest in IFR conditions.

Chart 2 below shows the distribution for fatal accidents. Here the twin engine aircraft represent only 32% of the sample, with the Cessna Twins appearing to suffer a higher proportion of fatalities.

The NTSB data has quite a high incidence of hard landings amongst the twins where structural icing was a probable factor. In addition, in the landing phase, poorly maintained boots and contaminated windscreens were a factor. However, the incidents related to hard landings and windscreen contamination were not fatal.

The single-engine sample has a much higher fatality rate, with over 70% occurring in the climb or cruise phase. Conversely, the majority of the twin fatalities were in the approach phase. A possible rationale may be that suitably equipped twins have the ability to carry a lot of ice in the cruise and descent, but as they change configuration for the approach they depart from controlled flight. In the case of singles, a high number of accidents in climb/cruise may reflect that they are not well equipped for FIKI, and are getting into serious problems before making it to the approach phase.

The AOPA ASF data sampling for all GA from 2003 through 2007 produced 13 fatal accidents, of which four were twins, two of them turbine (a Conquest and a King Air); showing that even turbine equipment is not immune to icing related fatalities. The nine fatal accidents related to singles covered: Beech 35/36, Cessna 182, Cirrus and a PA32. In total during the period there were 27 structural icing accidents in the GA fleet according to the ASF database. This appears to suggest that a relatively stable 50-70% fatality rate within the sample, with some bias towards fatalities in the single engine sample.

Structural icing does not rank high among the overall probable risk factors for GA accidents (probably less than 3% of accidents), but the fatality incidence and the persistent number of accidents (despite improvement in technology, e.g. TKS), requires proper planning to avoid icing encounters if possible. The number of accidents may also be understated. For example, when the Piper PA46 went through a comprehensive certification review in the late 1990s, one of the required safety improvements was to introduce automatic de-icing boot operation. This reflected certification concerns that some of the high altitude accidents were icing related. This safety measure for the PA46 may also appear consistent with high performance turbo-charged singles being caught out in icing conditions in the cruise.

The Aztec appears to have dropped out from the accident statistics in recent years, but this reflects a declining population of Aztecs being used in commercial/corporate operations. A previous sampling of the database only showed one fatality, for a non de-iced Aztec, and only seven accidents overall since 1960. While the Aztec has a good record, one cannot emphasize enough that the purpose of having de-icing equipment is to assist in leaving the icing area as quickly as possible.

Pre-flight preparation

LASORS (the UK CAA's pilot guide for operations) provides good advice on winter pre-flight checks, although the advice to melt stubborn ice on the aircraft with hot water is a recipe for potential re-freezing, and contamination of control linkages.

While the regulations provide that with a polished surface you might be legal to operate with some icing contamination, that view today might be considered incorrect. There are recorded accidents where polished flying surfaces resulted in flutter and structural damage to wing spars and ailerons and more recently there have been fatalities with turbine equipment taking off with minimal surface contamination.

If the outside temperature is below freezing and there is sufficient humidity, in my experience the only safe procedure to deal with stubborn ice contamination is a heated hangar and a thorough drying of the aircraft with a chamois leather. Using Type 1 de-icing fluid (other types are not authorised for GA piston aircraft), or an equivalent home brew with a pressure spray, may be an alternative. However, the holdover times for Type 1 in frost conditions is only 10-15 minutes and in freezing drizzle/rain less than three minutes. The best advice is that piston-engined aircraft should not depart in freezing drizzle/rain conditions and the accident statistics confirm this (the Aztec fatality mentioned above was a departure into freezing rain).

Protection against fuel icing

While not a structural icing condition, high altitude operations in very cold conditions can lead to fuel icing, especially with aircraft with bladder tanks where water might not be drained completely during the pre-flight check. Adding isopropyl alcohol (approximately one quart/25 US gallons) to prevent freezing of water contamination in the fuel is a sensible operating procedure – although care is required to achieve adequate mixing with the avgas.

Pre-flight testing of the de-ice equipment should be standard practice both in summer and winter. Pneumatic boots need to be conditioned with protective products as over time they suffer UV damage and an estimated useful life of 12 years for an unhangared aircraft is probably a fair estimate. Poorly maintained boots do fail asymmetrically, or provide marginal de-icing with significant degrading of any de-icing capability.

Flight planning

In flight planning the focus is on identifying weather which is likely to produce icing, understanding the geography of the route and how it might increase the exposure to icing, and ensuring a series of alternate plans to deal with icing. NASA produces a helpful web guide to planning the most effective diversions from icing conditions. This is aimed at the turbine commuter sector, which highlights that propeller aircraft, even turbines, need to plan to minimise exposure to icing (http://aircrafticing.grc.nasa.gov/courses.html).

What are the winter months?

Articles on icing invariably appear with seasonal predictability and refer to 'winter flying'. In the case of icing this is potentially misleading. Analysing longer run data for some GA aircraft, approximately 76% of icing related accidents occurred in the continental USA between November and March, and filtering the data for accidents in 'flat'/non-mountainous states, this increased to 87%. However, where orographic or lake/water effect might be a factor the distribution of accidents stretches from September through May, with one accident in Maine in June. In the author's experience it is not unusual to encounter icing conditions in August/September over continental Europe in typical GA flight levels – as Bordeaux is approximately on the same latitude as Maine this brings home that at least in Europe, icing is not only a 'winter flying' risk factor.

Weather

The 1975 edition of *Aviation Weather* (FAA EA-AC 00-6A) is still a reliable guide to icing with a complete chapter on the subject. It also identifies icing potential for different cloud types in the chapter for clouds. It is quite conservative in its identification of potential icing areas, highlighting that icing can and does occur in convective clouds at temperatures below -40°C. Where the NASA web resource advises that a 3,000 feet climb, or descent, in stratiform clouds should get you out of an icing area, the *Aviation Weather* advice is that while icing in stratiform clouds is rarely more than 5,000 feet thick, it can be much thicker in nimbostratus.

The other classic reference is the late Captain Robert Buck's *Weather Flying*, which teaches the concept of understanding the big picture in weather planning, and forming an understanding of the expected weather by following the developments of the main fronts and air masses over the days before a flight. Captain Buck is also quite sceptical of the real value of pneumatic boots other than a potential 'get out of jail' card when encountering icing conditions. In the case of the Aztec, which is FIKI-certified for light to moderate icing, the handbook was amended following the Roselawn ATR42 accident in 1994, to highlight the risk of supercooled large droplet icing (SLD) and to remind operators that the aircraft is not certified for flying in severe icing conditions. In effect the boots, even in good operating conditions, will not clear mixed icing efficiently and the unprotected areas soon cause a degradation in performance. The Aztec is draggy to say the least, but a 10-15 KIAS speed drop is not unusual in moderate icing conditions, and is an urgent signal to find warmer conditions.

On the day of the flight the significant weather charts help to identify the big picture and with the Airmet, provide an indication of areas where icing is expected and an estimate of the tops. An analysis of surface and temperatures aloft provides a picture of where icing is likely to occur, with 0° to -15°C being a high probability of icing for stratiform clouds and 0° to -20°C for convective clouds (but note comment on icing occurring at lower temperatures in the previous section). The theory that higher performance aircraft (170 KTAS) benefit from some compressibility heating effect is in the author's opinion wishful thinking. This does apply to jet aircraft, but the limited effect for piston aircraft is cancelled in lower pressure areas over airfoils and engine intakes where there would be a temperature drop.

The anti-icing windshield plate and heated props go on in the Aztec at +4°C where there is cloud, and the alternate air is cycled in cloud below freezing during FREDA checks (the pitot heat is on at take-off, and kept on throughout the flight). The freezing level in the southern half of the UK in winter seems to average between 2,000 and 5,000 feet. In the absence of frontal activity, tops are rarely above 7,000 to 10,000 feet. Ideally one should plan to depart with the knowledge that there is warm air at least up to the platform altitude for an approach. If, when in cloud, the icing is more severe than expected, then it would be a straightforward decision to return to base.

In reviewing the more recent accident series it was notable that single-engine aircraft appear to get into trouble in the departure/climb phase when encountering icing. While in a FIKI twin-engine (with both engines operating!) a departure through relatively low level freezing stratus might be considered if there is confidence the tops are reported around 5,000 or 6,000 feet, a FIKI single-engine might adopt more conservative criteria for attempting a departure climb on top through known icing clouds.

In the case of freezing rain or drizzle, the recommendation for piston-engined, and turbine aircraft without appropriate Type II de-icing treatment, is to wait for better conditions.

Frontal activity in the UK will easily take tops to FL180 in the winter with severe icing conditions in nimbostratus, and moderate icing in altostratus. Because the icing layer is extensive and thick the only options are to plan a route that avoids the worst of the frontal area (with a probable diversion of over a 100 miles), or to fly below the freezing level if this is above the minimum sector altitude (MSA).

The above would suggest that in an Aztec with known icing certification, a safe envelope is for departures in IMC where the freezing level is high enough to allow for a return approach in a warm air environment and tops are not above FL80. A departure into a frontal zone, or with the freezing level close to the ground, or where the typical airways altitude of FL80 – 120 will encounter moderate to severe icing with no possibility of climbing on top does not make the flight practicable. In certain circumstances a flight might be planned with an initial route away from forecast icing with tops above FL80, in a direction where expected tops are lower, which would allow a climb to a level above the tops expected in the original route. Once this height had been achieved the flight could resume the original planned route.

If there is the possibility of strong convective clouds then the rule is to be VMC and to avoid them. Embedded CBs in occluded fronts do occur in winter, especially in the UK, and they are no place for a light twin or single. In the late spring on occasion the Aztec has been flown through towering cumulus clouds at FL90, with tops of around FL110, and while it only took two or three minutes to fly through them, the de-icing boots had to work overtime. Best practice is to avoid towering cumulus and CBs visually or with radar.

On a long cross-country you are likely to cross part of a front, although hopefully you have planned to avoid the bulk of it and planned crossing at its weakest using the shortest route across (i.e. not flying parallel to the front). It is not unusual to be in the clear at FL90 but having to climb to FL120 or above to keep clear of cloud nearer the front or as you travel closer to the low. Ensuring oxygen availability is part of successful planning for icing.

Should I climb or should I descend?

Typically in stratocumulus, icing conditions are concentrated near the tops and while a FIKI-twin might climb on top it might produce some anxious moments (see Orographic lift below). The route might also be climbing up the slope of a warm front and therefore the 'climb on top' to escape an icing layer could literally take an eternity.

Conversely, the icing layer may stretch down to the MSA and beyond or there might be freezing rain below. This is why a careful analysis of the route and the weather, which builds in a series of well-thought alternates is necessary. Like in a game of chess, lack of planning several moves ahead can result in being caught between not been able to climb on top and rocks below.

The best margin of safety is to plan to have warm air or good VMC above the MSA and therefore the first out would be an ability to descend into warmer air above the MSA.

While a small layer of stratus with known tops, with some judgment, should not be an obstacle to an IFR flight, even turbine equipment are caught out trying to climb on top in more challenging conditions.

Orographic lift

US data appears to indicate that in mountain states there is a 70% fatality rate in icing encounters, with 50% of icing accidents in mountain states in the cruise phase. The accidents in the flat states were around 50% in the approach and landing phase (with a few related to obscured windscreens), while only 13% of the mountain states occurred in the approach/landing phase. However, 79% of the mountain accidents were in the en-route phase. There is probably an equipment bias in the data set as a lot of the mountain accidents were Turbo 210s without known icing certification. The message is clear: icing near mountains, and in particular on the windward side of the mountains, is probably more than any GA aircraft can cope with. Icing levels can easily reach FL180 and beyond, while the freezing level remains below the MEA or for that matter, MSA. Unlike stratiform clouds, the icing level where orographic lift is involved cannot be out-climbed by simply changing altitude by 3,000 feet to 5,000 feet. Most accidents in mountainous regions where icing was a factor appear to end in an unrecoverable loss of control.

The author has experienced a 'Never Again' flight having flown the Aztec across the Pyrenees and the Guadarrama mountains near Madrid. The orographic effect of the Pyrenees and the Basque mountains on a moist airflow from the Bay of Biscay led to much higher cloud tops than forecast. On this occasion near Pamplona the Aztec had to climb from FL110 (which had been forecast to be above the tops) to FL150 to remain clear of cloud. While the Aztec averaged around 200 – 300 fpm in the climb on-top (at an IAS of 130 mph which is used as the minimum climb speed in icing), the margin of safety, in retrospect, was not acceptable. With hindsight, a request for an approach to Pamplona as soon as it became obvious that the tops, and icing level, were above forecast, would have been wiser. However, Madrid was forecast as clear, hence the "press-on-itis".

Controllers have always been very helpful in clearing flights to different levels but it helps to mention that the flight level request is to avoid icing. In the event there is a delay in getting a level change, I recommended requesting an expedited level change and offering a heading change of 30°, and if this did not work then there is a need to declare an emergency. The Aztec being known-ice certified gives some extra comfort that declaring an emergency will not result in a possible regulatory review.

Alternate planning

Knowing where the warm air is, or where the conditions are clear, is an essential part of flying where there is a risk of an icing encounter. Preferably the destination and the alternates, including the take-off alternate, should have ILS as this should provide radar and a longer runway. Radar may come in handy if you need to descend below the MSA because you are carrying ice and the controller may guide you with radar vectoring to an area where there is a lower MSA and may also be able to expedite the approach. In the climb phase, the 180° turn back to the departure airport if icing, or the tops, are worse than expected is the first tactic. Staying on top in the en-route phase, and knowing that you are able to stay on top when flying towards a low, while monitoring alternates and destination, works en-route. A descent through icing needs to be planned. If the destination weather is not something you would depart into (frontal activity, freezing precipitation, airline PIREPs reporting moderate icing), then a diversion, and possibly a lengthy diversion, is required. As your TAS may be 10 or 20 knots slower due to icing, the need to carry more power, as well as the need for a lengthy diversion all suggest very conservative fuel planning. Several of the icing related accidents were due to fuel exhaustion.

Approach and landing

If there is ice on the wing, or the approach is in icing conditions, then a no flaps approach may be advisable and hence the longer runway of an ILS-equipped airport may be an advantage. The author has never carried out an approach where there were icing conditions in the approach phase although the Aztec has carried ice on the wings during the approach, which in due course melted off. (The boots will not totally eliminate mixed ice). Most of the accidents in the approach/landing phase were due to windscreen obscuration, poor visibility due to freezing fog or snow, or landing on taxiways instead of runways!

Departures from controlled flight due to icing in the approach phase may be due to a tail stall. As the elevator/stabilator has a smaller radius wing, and the angle of attack increases to the elevator/stabilator when flaps are extended, there is a risk of tail-stall in the approach phase when ice contamination is present – and the recovery drill is nearly always the inverse to a wing stall. The key recovery actions are a retraction of flaps, increase of power and raising the nose to reduce the angle of attack on the tail.

Conclusion

If you plan carefully and have a clear idea of the circumstances where you will cancel the flight or divert, then a light twin with known icing certification can safely operate in certain icing conditions. The excess power of the second engine, and the de-icing and anti-icing equipment, allow you to leave the icing area - not to allow you to loiter or make the controllers' life easy. There is more weather analysis to be done, with more alternates required than a typical IMC flight, and your route should avoid areas of icing caused by orographic lift, or frontal areas where there are embedded convective clouds or extensive severe icing in nimbostratus and altostratus. Knowing where the warm or clear air is and being able to reach it promptly is essential.

AOPA provides a very good safety briefing for winter flying (www.aopa.org/asf/publications/sa11.pdf) and this is highly recommended.

SECTION 3
Operational matters

SECTION 4

Touring

Section Contents

Close up view of the Matterhorn by **PPL/IR Europe** member Peter Holy in his TB20 Trinidad

PA46 Malibu at Gibraltar by **PPL/IR Europe** member David Findon

Piper PA23 Aztec owned by **PPL/IR Europe** member Timothy Nathan at Resolute Bay in Canada, demonstrating the ultimate achievement for a light aircraft on an epic tour around the North Pole

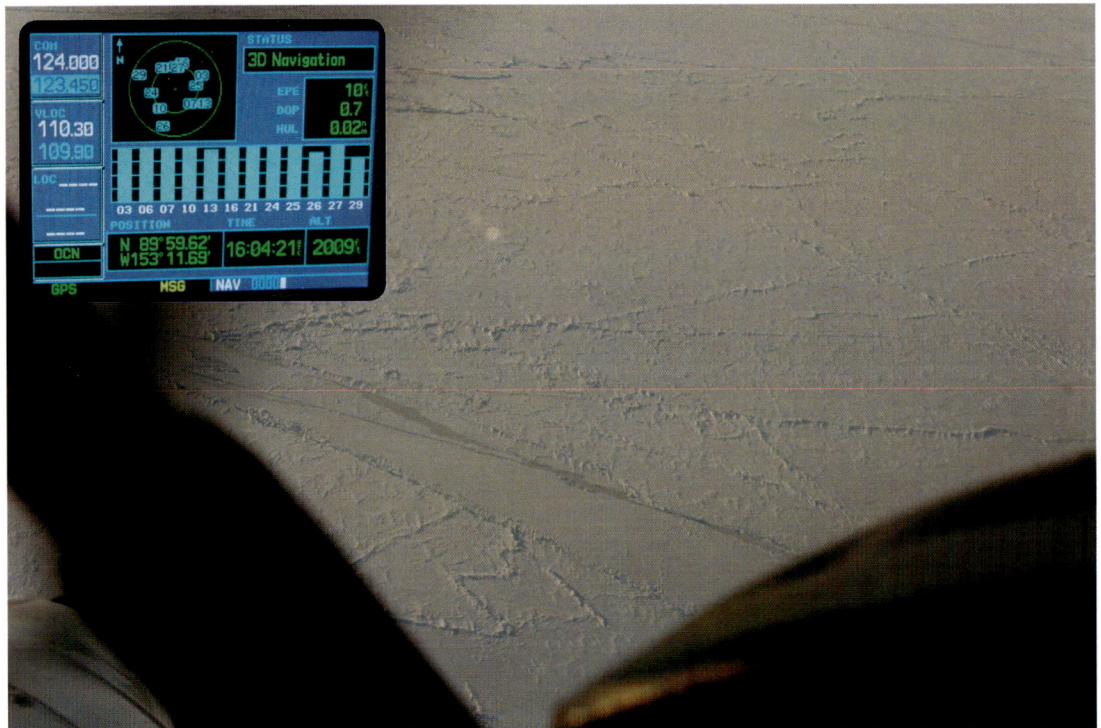

Frozen arctic, with GPS inset showing arrival at the North Pole, by Timothy Nathan

Rugged landscape of northern Canada, by Timothy Nathan

Flying low out of Spitsbergen in northern Norway, by Timothy Nathan

PPL/IR Europe member Steve Copeland on a Standard Instrument Departure from Halifax to Moncton in Canada

Photo supplied by *PPL/IR Europe* member Phil Wadsworth with American General AG-5B at Albi, France enroute to Croatia in 2004

New terminal and control tower under construction at Brac airport in Croatia, on return from a **PPL/IR Europe** trip to the Greek islands in 2005. Photo Sally Turner

Photo supplied by **PPL/IR Europe** member Cameron Aitken with Piper Arrow II at Sarajevo

PPL/IR Europe members Stephen and Judith Niechcial in their Gulfstream American AA5B Tiger at Calvi. Photo by Sally Turner

PPL/IR Europe member Jeff Pearce departing Calvi in PA28 Cherokee Arrow. Photo by Sally Turner

Refuelling in Tunis on *PPL/IR Europe* trip in 2006. Photo Sally Turner

Aircraft parking outside the self catering chalets at Eremo della Giubliana on the *PPL/IR Europe* trip to Sicily. Photo Judith Niechcial

PPL/IR Europe member Steve Copeland on the ILS to Guernsey after breaking cloud at 700'

Returning home, inbound to Southend. Photo Sally Turner

1 *PPL/IR Europe* fly out to Tunisia and Sicily 2006

By Jeff Pearce

The aircraft taking part in this trip comprised a brace each of TB20s, AA5s and Mooneys, a Bonanza, a Seneca and a Cessna 303 and me in an Arrow.

Being an airways-based trip, all aircraft were airways equipped but in addition most had IFR approved GPS (mainly Garmin 430s) as well as autopilots of some sort and most importantly, as it proved, stormscopes. However, my much loved Arrow had only an autopilot, though it did have a turbo so there was at least the possibility of flying above weather that may have defeated the normal aspirated engined participants.

Well prior to the start we all received information packs with details of the planned route, hotels booked, etc., thereby taking away a lot of the worries for neophyte long distance flyers – like me!

The event was due to start on Saturday 17 June at Calvi, Corsica (LFKC) with us all making our own way there, but quite a few decided to start earlier, with an overnight stop en-route, in our case at Grenoble (LFLS), as did three other crews.

Friday: Bournemouth (EGHH) to Grenoble (LFLS)
Checking the weather on Friday morning showed light winds and good conditions across most of France except for the last part of the journey which gave OCNL CB

from 4,000 feet and a SIGMET reporting TS observed in the area of St. Etienne. The Grenoble TAF was giving few CB at 4,000 feet, recent rain and TS. Not having equipment to help out with potentially 'iffy' weather I try never to fly in IMC if CB's and TS are forecast, as my only way of avoiding them is to see them first. A VFR flight offered the possibility of getting there, albeit that rising ground between Roanne and Vienne would require an MSA of 4,500 feet which, given the forecast of CB's at 4,000 feet, seemed to indicate that Roanne would be as far as we would get, but at least we would be on our way. A revised VFR flight plan was drawn up and filed with Heathrow, GenDec faxed, NOTAMS checked and we were ready to go.

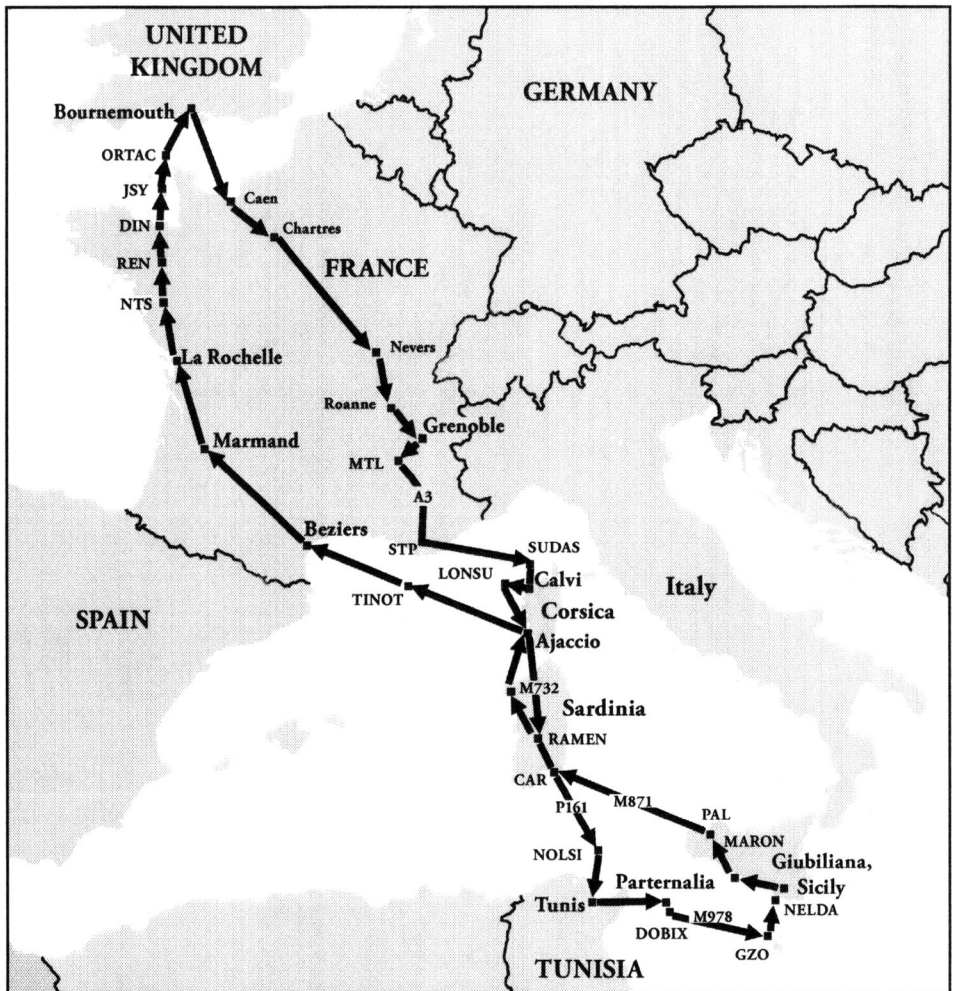

Figure 1. Route of the *PPL/IR Europe* group fly out to Tunisia and Sicily

To give credit to the Met boys, the weather ran exactly to forecast with the majority of the journey very pleasant. Beyond Roanne the weather began to deteriorate but we were able to climb to 4,500 feet in VMC, to clear the higher ground ahead. The weather to our right around St Etienne was decidedly unfriendly with black clouds, heavy rain and lightning, whilst to our left a smaller cell was doing its bit to dampen the parched French countryside and spitting out the occasional lightning as well. Fortunately, just slightly left of track there was a large clear area between the two cells and we could see clear air beyond the ridge, so we headed for that only to be greeted by lightning discharging to earth on the ridge directly where we were heading. I reasoned that having just discharged, that particular cloud was unlikely to discharge again immediately afterwards, so we went for it and after just a couple of minutes buttock-clenching flight, came out the other side of the rising ground to beautiful weather and a visual approach to Grenoble on a hot but calm evening.

Saturday: Grenoble to Calvi, Corsica (LFKC)

Meteo provided a full written briefing with the unpleasant news that whilst the weather at Grenoble and Calvi was CAVOK, there were embedded CB's and TS forecast and observed on the section MTL to STP. The forecaster offered the opinion that this weather would move northeast and weaken over the next two hours. So whilst the other three stormscope-equipped crews prepared to depart, we opted to file IFR for a departure two hours later, giving us approximately three hours before we would be in the region of the current weather. Third to take off was the Mooney, taking off about thirty minutes before our departure time.

All went well until reaching PERUS. As we progressed south we became IMC at FL110 and it became increasingly turbulent and then the rain started. Clearly the weather had not moved out of the way as forecast. As it became darker and the rain increased ATC were kept busy by the 'heavy metal' requesting vectors left and right to try and avoid the worst of the weather. We could also hear the Mooney crew requesting vectors trying to pick their way through. Without stormscope and with hindsight, maybe we should have turned back but St Tropez looked invitingly close, where a descent out of the weather was possible, so we continued, although when lightning flashed in front of us I questioned the wisdom of that decision.

From St Tropez a descent to F060 and VMC resulted in a pleasant crossing of the Med to Calvi for a LOC/DME approach to runway 18. With a 3 kt tail wind and over 7,500 feet of runway, some opted for a straight in approach, while others broke off for a visual to 36. The approach into Calvi is interesting with high ground immediately right and left of the runway and a mountain dead ahead! As a result the Missed Approach Point (MAP) is 3.4 miles for Cat A aircraft, 4.2 miles for Cat C. Commercials landing on 36 have to break off from an 18 instrument approach and fly a visual circuit outside of the high ground before turning base to pick their way between that and the mountain, to line up on 36.

A short taxi ride brought us to Hotel Le Belvedere in Calvi, close to the port and beach. Our room had a perfect view of The Citadel (the old fortified town) with the sea and the mountains in the background. That evening the group met up for a sundowner and a meal together which quickly became the norm and was a very enjoyable part of the trip as it gave me the opportunity to discuss aviation with other "airheads" while my long suffering wife talked "girly things" with the other long suffering wives and girlfriends.

Sunday

Sunday was a free day, this being the general format: one day flying, one day sightseeing.

Monday Calvi, to Tunis, Tunisia (DTTA)

We were number three to depart and whereas the previous two got an AJO5C SID off runway 36 and straight out over the sea, we got an AJO5C off runway 18. This gave me two problems, never faced before. Firstly how do you get onto a northerly SID when using a southerly runway; the Jeppesen plate gave no indication on this. Secondly how to avoid the mountain staring us in the face! A maximum rate of climb on take off and a right turn avoiding the worst of the high ground to the west of the runway, with a 180 back over the field to pick up the SID seemed the only option, so we advised ATC of our intentions and as they offered no objections or alternatives that is what we did, clearing the high ground by enough to be safe but any sort of engine problem on the climb out would have left us with very few options.

The flight down to Tunis was straightforward at FL110 apart from strong downdraughts over Sardinia with close to 1,000 fpm on the VSI on occasions, which made height keeping difficult. We also had the added annoyance that the autopilot had gone u/s on the climb out from Calvi, leaving us with nearly three and a half hours hand flying the aircraft in what was effectively IMC. Although all airfields en-route were reporting CAVOK, at FL110, whilst you could often make out the ground below, in front it was either cloud or so extremely hazy there was never an horizon to level on. In these conditions relaxing the instrument scan was not an option; it was to be a long flight.

The arrival into Tunis was a bit confused with some of us getting an ILS to runway 19, which we had no plates for. However, ATC were very helpful and assisted with vectors. Once on the localiser the runway was clearly visible from over ten miles out. On landing the OAT was forty degrees and by the time we had taxied to Tunisavia, our handling agents, we were like a 'limp lettuce'. Fuel had been arranged through Tunisavia and based on our anticipated requirements, Tunisavia had pre-ordered the requisite number of barrels, avgas not being normally available at Tunis. Having to hand pump the fuel over took the refuellers some time. Unfortunately, the full quantity we had ordered had not arrived and some mutual rationing had to take place to ensure we would all have enough to reach Sicily which would be the next 'watering hole' for the aircraft, otherwise it would mean a divert to Malta.

Once four of us were refuelled we taxied behind a 'follow me' van to the apron in front of the freight terminal. A bus then took us back to an air-conditioned office, which was a welcome relief from the searing heat outside. When the next contingent had refuelled and taxied out to the apron, their pick up driver insisted that they had to go to the main terminal building, which effectively meant our party was now split. In this atmosphere rumours start easily and at one stage we heard that the contingent in the main terminal were being questioned by police. Needless to say, the rumours were all false but it did add a certain frisson to our situation. It also meant that by the time we got away the first to arrive had been stuck there for over three hours!

We were booked into the Hotel Sidi Bou Said in the pretty, small town of the same name just outside Tunis. This proved to be excellent with a pool and scenic views over Tunis.

Tuesday

A tour guide and coach had been arranged for the day. In the morning we went to Carthage to see the Roman and Carthaginian ruins and then in the afternoon we went to the Medina, the old walled town, although virtually all of the original city walls were destroyed during the Second World War. We then went into the souk, a covered market, where you can buy just about anything and while there, we had a traditional Tunisian meal at a four hundred-year-old large house now converted to an excellent restaurant. The heat of the afternoon led most back to the air conditioned hotel, with the pilots pleading the need of having to file flight plans for the next day. Using the service www.homebriefing.com, these were filed via a laptop.

Wednesday Flight 1: Tunis to Pantelleria (LICG)

In view of the short distance and blue skies it was decided to keep this leg simple with "VFR, DCT" being the only entry needed on the flight plan. Departing Tunis VFR there is a visual departure route, initially heading southeast and at predetermined height. Simply taking off and heading straight towards LICG is not wise given the large prohibited area due east of the field. The visual route runs via points CE1 and then CE, both not above 1,000 feet and then we were told to expect a routing CE direct to the CBN VOR not above 1,500 feet, interesting given the high ground en-route to over 1,300 feet! In practice we were cleared to our flight planned altitude almost immediately on passing CE and well before the rising ground approaching CBN. Then followed an uneventful short over-water flight to Pantelleria before joining right-hand down wind for runway 26.

With us all landed, the Italian bureaucracy kicked in. This stop was intended to be a quick lunch break and whistle stop tour of this small island, but police and customs had other ideas. At first they wanted to check all our bags, and the first couple of aircraft got a full check, after which they cut it back to a quick cursory check of one bag of their choice from each aircraft. We were then allowed to continue, but only as far as airside in the terminal building, where the police amused themselves going through our passports and arrival paperwork. Two hours later we were free to go, whereupon a mini-bus appeared to whisk us off to a local restaurant. On piling aboard it became apparent that there were not enough seats, quickly overcome by the simple expedient of adding a couple of plastic garden chairs in the space adjacent to the sliding door!

The staff at the restaurant were unphased by the sudden appearance of 20 hot and sweaty aircrew demanding a meal and very quickly produced an excellent fish meal but dessert was declined due to time pressure and it was back on the bus to the airfield. This was a pity because we would have liked to see more of this isolated Italian outpost. The problem then was getting airside once more. The best the police could offer was that we would be delayed 'no more than about half an hour' while they waited for one of their officers to return from the police station with an additional form which we had to fill in. Pleading filed flight plans fell on deaf ears and it looked like we were going nowhere. However, in our faltering Italian we established that the forms needed were the ones we had already filled in on landing, but these had not been passed onto the police, who could not let us go as a result. So – find the forms, problem solved! Well not exactly, each form needed to be married up with its relevant passport. They had all twenty forms and all twenty passports but seemed incapable of putting the two together. Fortunately, one of our number took control of the situation, taking both forms and passports off of the police officer holding them, and then proceeded to give them back to him in matched pairs. To the officer's astonishment he realised that they did indeed match and we were on our way – but not all of us. On taxying out, the Bonanza's alternator went off-line and its crew forced to stay put. What a place to breakdown, stuck on a small, dormant volcanic island halfway between Africa and Sicily with nothing in the way of local engineering facilities.

Wednesday Flight 2: Pantelleria to Giubiliana, Ragusa, Sicily

Apart from having to leave one of our aircraft behind, the departure from Pantelleria was uneventful with an initial clearance to 5,000 feet, which before reaching was revised to FL100. Routing via GZO was an indirect routing to Giubiliana but was the best airways routing we could get. However, on reaching DOBIX we were instructed 'route direct NELDA' which cut a large corner off. On approaching NELDA we asked Malta ATC for a descent but were advised that this could not be given until reaching NELDA. With the group's aircraft arriving at NELDA between FL100 and FL120, and twelve miles between NELDA and Giubiliana, clearly we were going to be a tad high on arrival in the overhead!

Our stay at Giubiliana was the high point of the holiday; staying at The Eremo della Giubiliana a former 14th century convent, now converted to a five star hotel complete with its own airfield. Even better, there are five holiday cottages adjacent to the runway giving some of us the opportunity of waking up in the morning with the other love of our life parked at the end of the garden! But first we had to land.

Although nothing had been said, I suspect some, if not all, of the pilots in the group had been thinking about this approach for some time. The runway is 680 metres long, 10 metres wide with a stonewall at one end and an escarpment at the other. Landing long or short wasn't an option and the slope of the runway dictated landings on 07, take offs from 25, whatever the wind direction. We had been advised to arrive early or late in the day as thermal activity invariably gave strong cross winds on the plateau on which the airfield is sited. High ambient temperature and 1,400 feet altitude all conspired to make this an interesting approach and departure. We were number four to arrive and our experience was typical. Having landed safely, the wonderful surroundings, peace and tranquillity mixed with a sense of relief, meant that we were all grinning like Cheshire cats. But then the sound of the cicadas and bird song would be interrupted by the sound of a Lycoming at high level and looking up we would see the next aircraft approaching, struggling to lose as much height as possible before circling over the field in a long and protracted descent. At this stage, those on the ground would switch their attention to watching the next arrival; it was like having your own mini-airshow! Each safe arrival was greeted with a round of applause from those on the ground and a sigh of relief from the pilot. Fortunately all the landings were uneventful, although we did a go round with the Arrow as we were a bit fast on short final and one of the AA5's disappeared out of sight below the escarpment and level of the runway for a heart-stopping moment before popping up again, to go on and execute a greaser of a landing right on the numbers!

Thursday – Saturday

The Hotel Erema della Giubiliana would make a stunning location for anyone, but especially those able to arrive by air. The main building is steeped in history. A former 12th century Arabic fortified structure it became a convent in the 14th century before being used by the Knights of The Order of St. John in the 16th century, finally becoming the private residence of the Nifosi family in the 18th century, who still own it to this day and have recently opened the property as a hotel. This has been completed with sensitivity and without detracting from the natural charm of the place. A visit is highly recommended but if not current in short field landings, do go and practice a few before arrival at Giubiliana.

As we were to be here until Sunday, the Cessna 303 crew flew back to Pantelleria to pick up the Bonanza crew who were endeavouring to get an alternator from the UK and an engineer from Malta to Pantelleria to complete the repair over the next couple of days. We did the tourist bit, including a trip up Etna but, as Saturday drew to a close we started to address the question of filing flight plans for the start of the journey back home.

There had been three flights out of Giubiliana while we were there. All three flights had some difficulties in opening their flight plans on departing this VFR field. In theory, Catania was the obvious choice to call, but although only about thirty miles away there are known comms difficulties which can prevent radio calls getting through below F090. Second choice would be Campo radar but even that couldn't be guaranteed and as most of us would be heading northwest, Palermo seemed a good back up. Who to file the flight plan with was also a consideration. On one of the earlier flights the crew filed using www.homebriefing.com. However, when they did manage to contact Catania they denied having the flight plan and left them to circle to 10,000 feet over the field while they sorted it out, and before giving them their clearance. The moral of this seemed to be to file with Catania so I phoned my flight plan with them direct.

After a final excellent meal together to mark the end of the tour, an early night was in order as we had an early start the next day to get off while it was still comparatively cool and calm, with some planning a long day's flying.

Sunday: Giubiliana to Ajaccio, Corsica (LFKJ)

After the challenge of getting into Giubiliana, getting out again was a comparative 'doddle' with a downhill departure from runway 25. Our VFR departure as far as MARON meant we were able to climb to 5,500 feet before opening the flight plan. Despite waiting to gain altitude it proved impossible to raise Catania and we switched frequency to Campo radar who replied immediately and opened our flight plan, before quickly passing us on to Rome who cleared us to FL110 direct Trapani and then direct KAPIL, which would cut a few miles off the route. On approaching KAPIL, another aircraft joined us on track to CAR in our 11 o'clock and a thousand feet below us. This was one of the Mooneys. Had they known we were there, it might have given them some reassurance on the 185-mile sea crossing to Sardinia but they were unaware of our watching presence behind them and by the time we were over Sardinia they had crept ahead and disappeared from view.

The crossing of Sardinia proved uneventful and a lot less 'lumpy' than on the way down but on reaching the Med between Sardinia and Corsica we went IMC with a lot of turbulence and rain. There had been no forecast of CBs or TS activity so we were pretty confident it wouldn't be much. Throughout our journey the OAT had been around 4-5 degrees positive, but on going IMC it dropped to minus 2. Fortunately we saw no ice, but it continued to be a turbulent crossing for the next 10 minutes. On landing at Ajaccio we taxied to the pumps to find the Mooney and the Seneca both in front of us. Both reported a smooth crossing at FL100 as did the TB20 crew at FL190 so we had obviously drawn the short straw at FL110!

Originally several of us had intended to land at Olbia in Sardinia to refuel but the imposition of a 150 Euro 'luxury' tax on all visiting aircraft and yachts meant a change of plan. Doubtless some bureaucrat is patting himself on the back at having found a way of raising extra revenue. The reality is that instead of getting our landing fees, fuel, meals and hotel spending they got precisely nothing and doubtless others will come to the same conclusion. Not a help for their tourism industry!

The Seneca flew on to Lyon Bron with one of the Bonanza crew to meet up with the now repaired Bonanza. The TB20 and Mooney routed to overnight in Switzerland dodging thunderstorm activity. We decided to overnight in Ajaccio.

Monday: Ajaccio to Beziers (LFMU)

Having completed the TINOT3P SID and cleared to F080 we continued en-route towards the radio fix TINOT where we anticipated a turn towards the Martiques VOR (MTG) as per the airway, instead of which we got 'route direct ZR' the locator NDB for Beziers. This meant an almost straight line route AJO to ZR. On the down-side it would also mean being over water the whole time apart from the couple of miles coasting in at Beziers. On approaching ZR, the airfield was clearly visible through the heat haze, so we cancelled IFR for a VFR approach to runway 10.

Tuesday: Beziers to Hurn (EGHH)

We planned to fly back to Bournemouth in the day, airways via La Rochelle (LFBH) but a check on Avbrief showed yet more CB and TS activity around Bordeaux. After our experiences battling CBs and TS while IMC approaching St Tropez on the way out, my previously held rule not to fly IFR when CBs and TS are likely seemed a wise one and so we planned the route to La Rochelle VFR.

Once again thunderstorm activity caused us problems and we made an intermediate landing at Marmande (LFDM) to wait for weather clearance before proceeding to La

Rochelle.

The visual approach to La Rochelle was straightforward and we were instructed to join via the bridge for a downwind right hand to runway 28, and landed for hopefully the penultimate time on this trip. After refuelling and a pleasant meal in the airport restaurant we filed a flight plan for home.

Although we filed VFR for the final leg to Hurn, it seemed unlikely that we would be able to get all the way home VFR due to Jerseys METAR of SCT 800 feet, but as there was no mention of CBs or TS, if the cloud defeated us, we could always upgrade to IFR. When the last of the 'foreign' controllers passed us on to Jersey it was a welcome change to hear an easily understood voice return our call and a prompt clearance through their zone direct ORTAC at 3,000 feet. We continued in beautiful sunshine and all went well until approaching ORTAC when it became obvious we would be going IMC at that level, and a request for a change to an IFR clearance to Jersey Zone was granted immediately. We had visualised approaching the coast with Bournemouth bathed in sunshine, the chalk cliffs of Swanage to our left, and the Needles to our right, but instead, we were IMC until a vectored ILS to runway 26 saw us dropping out of the gloom with about five miles to run. Finally we were home after a most memorable holiday and a real sense of accomplishment.

SECTION 4
Touring

168

2 IFR trip from Shoreham, UK to Prague, Czech Republic

By Peter Holy

This article describes an IFR (airways) flight from Shoreham (EGKA) to Prague (LKPR), done in 2006. The intention is to show the essence of the IFR flight planning process, for a representative flight in the European airways system, in a non-deiced aircraft with oxygen and a 20,000 foot ceiling - a Socata TB20.

Pilot: FAA CPL/IR, 900 hrs total time. The aircraft is on the U.S. (N) register.

Route planning

As with all IFR flights outside the UK, an ICAO flight plan must be filed and this is done via the Eurocontrol system. There are various ways to develop an IFR routing which is acceptable to the Eurocontrol computer; the simplest way is to try the free and unofficial "ASA" website used by flight simulation enthusiasts http://rfinder. asalink.net/free/. Entering EGKA LKPR, altitude between FL080 and FL160, Low Level airways, and selecting the "RAD", "CDR" and "Use Daily CRAM" checkboxes generated the route: MAY R8 DVR L9 KONAN L607 RUDUS L984 SULUS Z650 TIPAM Z35 LOMKI, which was copied into the Eurocontrol route validation website www.cfmu.eurocontrol.be/j_cia_public/cia_public/pages/ifpuv-structured.jsf and generated the much sought after NO ERRORS message. Often, the initially generated route does not validate and one has to go to the bottom of the ASA page and check the various restriction violations which it puts up and re-route. It is an iterative process which usually works eventually. More route planning methods are discussed here: www.peter2000.co.uk/aviation/ifr-flying/ifr-flying.html.

Unfortunately one cannot load an airways route directly into a GPS - unless it is one of the models that support named airway routes such as a Garmin 480. Any older GPS has to be loaded with the waypoints that make up the route. One can get the waypoints by picking them off the route on the paper IFR chart, or one can do it by generating a "plog" (a list of waypoints with headings, etc) with the Jeppesen FliteStar IFR flight planning program, using its Plain Text route specification function (in the routepack wizard function). (Jeppview 3 has the same plain text input in its routepack wizard but it doesn't call it that; the plain text input is the default mode). This also generates a picture of the route and you can print off various chart sections (which, assuming you have a current database, avoids the need to spread the paper charts all over the cockpit) and the flight plan to be filed, etc. My GPS is a KLN94 which, like all the old-generation units, does not accept direct airways-name entry; moreover it has a 20-waypoint limit per flight plan which can be fun on some routes. Obviously one needs to load all waypoints at which an airway changes direction; it is debatable whether one needs to load in those where it does not but doing so can be helpful if ATC give you a DCT to one of them. ATC often issue shortcuts and they generally prefer waypoints which lie on one's filed route.

The ICAO flight plan can now be filed using any means available to the pilot for filing flight plans. I use the Vienna ATC facility Homebriefing www.homebriefing.com which at reasonable cost will accept flight plans for flights wholly outside its own country (unlike all other known website flight plan filing facilities). This is a fantastic service, allowing you to online edit the flight plan right up to the departure, change its time, etc. For this trip, the IFR flight plan was filed without the "IFPS ROUTE AMENDMENT ACCEPTED" option, which is popular with some pilots, and was accepted without modification.

Unlike with VFR flight plans, there is no need to specify time estimates to national boundaries. The whole flight is seamless, with handovers from one control sector to the next. Individual countries within Europe become unimportant. Controlled airspace considerations are also irrelevant; most or all of the route will be in controlled airspace anyway. Restricted/prohibited areas also do not matter - ATC should not knowingly direct you into one of those.

It is advisable to check that the route will pass the Eurocontrol check at different flight levels, from the lowest (which lies below the 0°C level and which one might therefore fly if encountering icing) right up to the aircraft operating ceiling. My general strategy in IFR is to climb until VMC on top is reached and then ask ATC for a "stop climb". This results in a pleasant flight which, except for the climb and descent phases, is free of icing and turbulence. When ATC grants the request, they usually ask whether you want to change your filed level to this level, and the best answer is "Yes". However, one needs to be a little careful if a higher level to cross a specific piece of airspace is needed later on; if for example you have levelled off at FL100 and your filed route crosses the

Frankfurt TMA which requires FL130+ then you may get a dogleg when you get there. In such a scenario it is worth telling ATC that you can climb to FL130 as required.

As I was going to fly back the following day, I also wanted to work out the return route and file a flight plan for it. This route proved to be a lot harder and I was unable to get anything out of the ASA website that was acceptable to CFMU; checking off the various route violations in the ASA site only generated yet more route violations. At the time of writing, Prague used to be one of the hardest routes to work out (it is fine now). Eventually I capitulated and emailed CFMU who very helpfully returned a viable route as described on page 175 below.

Weather planning

IFR weather planning differs from VFR.

An instrument capable and experienced pilot in a well equipped aircraft can generally fly "VFR" in atrocious weather provided he remains below the cloud base, or provided he can fly VMC on top with a virtual certainty of a clear sky at the destination – though obviously this needs to be done within airspace which is either uncontrolled (G) or within which a transit can be granted by ATC.

With IFR, the weather strategy needs to be smarter. One is flying at airway MEAs (minimum enroute altitudes) and in Europe these are usually high enough to place you potentially in both cloud and above the 0°C level – icing! - and nobody likes sitting in IMC anyway. Contrary to what most VFR pilots think, the objective in IFR is to fly in VMC – and due to minimum airway levels this usually means above the clouds rather than below them. While ATC will always (but sometimes not immediately) allow you to escape dangerous weather or airframe icing, the aircraft may not have the performance to get out of it. Flying along in IMC at -8°C until the aircraft is covered in ice and starts to lose performance, and only then asking ATC for a descent or a climb, is not the way to do it. Another factor is that if you have been flying in IMC for some time, you have no idea of the height of the tops above you, so asking for a climb through what may be 15,000 feet of freezing cloud could be really dumb. One therefore needs to think ahead, climb above any cloud if at all possible, and keep all the options open.

The first thing to check was the MSLP (mean sea level pressure) chart. For the date of flight, this showed high pressure over southern UK; this would generally mean good clear weather but it could also mean widespread low cloud or fog, so additional information would be required.

The strategy which different pilots apply depends on their attitude to risk and their willingness/ability to deal with icing and turbulence. The decision is often influenced by passengers being carried, if any. I would generally not fly through a front if I was likely to be in IMC, so scattered CBs are OK provided there is no organised thick cloud layer which is too thick to climb on top of. A front in IMC at the departure/destination can be a real problem because then one has to climb/descend through it.

So, the next thing to establish was the likely vertical extent (bases and tops) of the cloud cover. This was to ensure, as far as possible, that the flight would be in VMC, or at least below or above the layer with icing potential (roughly 0°C to -15°C). For VFR flight, the obvious way to get the bases is a list of TAFs for airports along the route, but this easy option will be available at most 24 hours ahead. Unfortunately TAFs provide no clue to cloud tops, or to the existence of additional layers above the reported base which itself could be something rather benign. A base of FEW030 looks nice for a VFR flight below 3,000 feet (above the aerodrome level) provided this is above the MSA, but is of no use for an airways flight at FL100 if there is a solid layer from 6,000 feet to 20,000 feet and the freezing (0°C) level is at 8,000 feet! Cloud bases above 5,000 feet AAL may also not be reported in TAFs or METARs.

To get an idea of the vertical profile of the atmosphere you need to look at a forecast tephigram. For the outbound route, this showed a likely cloud layer between 750mb and 650mb i.e. (very roughly) 9,000 to 11,000 feet. The website these forecasts come from is http://my.meteoblue.com/my/ - look under Meteogram/Soundings. Importantly, the 0°C level was around 700mb (10,000 feet) which was satisfactory relative to the available airway levels (basically anything above FL080, or lower if you really need it and there are no terrain issues) and the aircraft operating ceiling which is about 18,000 feet (500mb) in the Trinidad.

Additional data comes from the SigWx form. Form 415 (a version of the UK Form 215) is of limited use at airway levels.

I am not a weather expert and do my best to interpret the data I can get. If in doubt I telephone a professional forecaster on a premium-rate number.

Other Requirements

One needs to get NOTAMs. ICAO requires a pilot to use the briefing facility provided by the country of departure. Theoretically an aircraft with sufficient range could fly any route starting in the UK so I use the UK www.ais.org.uk website and the Narrow Route Briefing. One should enter the flight planned route; that should flag up relevant en-route factors like an out of service VOR. The value of the en-route data is slightly debatable since (under ATS control) one probably won't fly the exact filed route anyway. However, the really important stuff is at the end; for example on a recent flight (Berlin Tempelhof) I found the ILS and VOR out of service, leaving just the NDB approaches available.

I never use airport weather briefing services. I carry a PDA and a laptop with a tri-band GPRS/3G adaptor and can get conventional internet access on those. GPRS works reliably throughout Europe and the USA. The laptop can also send faxes which is very useful for "prior notice" airports, often a common requirement around Europe.

In the UK, one has to fax the General Aviation Report form to one or more of Police, Immigration, and Customs authorities. In this case (Shoreham Airport) I needed to notify Immigration only of the return flight. Prague has 24hr Customs, whose notice is satisfied by the filing of the ICAO flight plan.

I use oxygen anywhere at or above FL100, utilising a portable oxygen kit purchased from the USA. This is essential for flight at European airway levels. The oxygen flow rate increases with altitude and this becomes a flight planning issue: one will choose a lower level if going away on a long trip. On this trip, this was not an issue since there was no way for me (flying alone) to use up the whole bottle - even if I did the whole trip at the aircraft ceiling of 18,000-20,000 feet.

Flight EGKA-LKPR

The outbound filed route was MAY R8 DVR L9 KONAN L607 RUDUS L984 SULUS Z650 TIPAM Z35 LOMKI, as shown below:

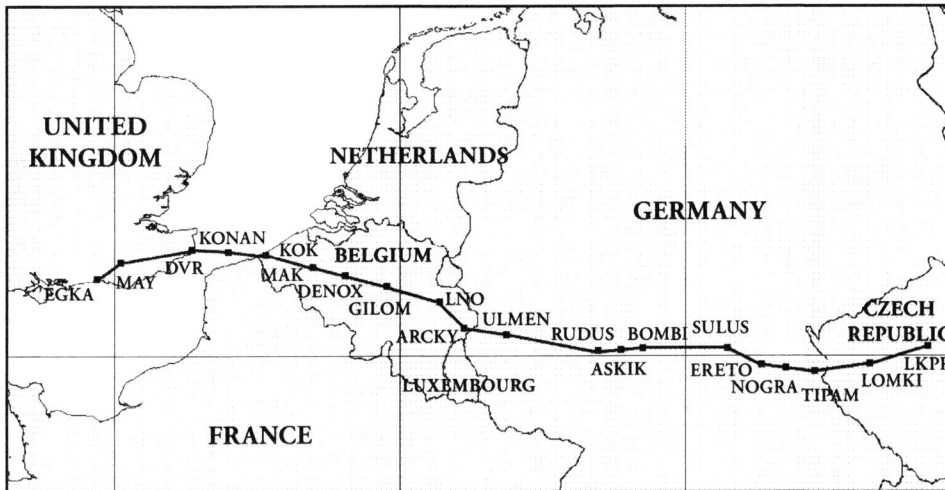

Upon sight of a IFR/airways flight plan, Shoreham ATC will phone up the first IFR sector (London Control) and obtain a provisional IFR departure clearance, comprising of an initial route (always remaining outside controlled airspace), a transponder code, and the first IFR sector frequency to contact. You then collect this clearance before lining up on the runway, in the normal "Nxxxxx ready to copy departure clearance" manner.

I had planned for a 12:00Z departure but a few hours beforehand received an email and a SMS message from Homebriefing advising me that a slot time had been allocated for 12:10Z, due to traffic density. Not a big deal at all – some slots can cause much longer delays.

I got airborne with a clearance of DCT MAY, climb 2400ft, remain outside controlled airspace, squawk 0516, contact London Control 133.17. London gave me a DCT SFD FL080, HDG 105° after SFD so the filed flight plan did not last longer than the first radio call.

After that I got a long string of instructions comprising of vectors or DCTs or "own navigation to XXX". Occasionally I was given a DCT waypoint which happened to be on my filed route. As usual on airways flights, the entire flight was a straightforward RNAV point-to-point navigation exercise based around airways intersections and thus very difficult without an IFR GPS. Many of the waypoints given are too far away for the old-style RNAV product (e.g. a KNS80) to work; for example I was given DCT ODOMO from 115nm away and a KNS80 would have not had VOR/DME reception from that distance. In practice one also tunes in any VOR/DME one can find on the route.

Overall, the actual route flown corresponded well with the filed route. I filed for FL130 but before reaching FL110 I asked for a stop climb at FL110. This conserved oxygen and probably gave me a slightly better speed. However, 60nm before Frankfurt airspace I was asked to climb FL130 or accept a detour, since FL130 was the lowest acceptable over Frankfurt. I replied "it will be a slow climb, about 300fpm" and he replied "fine, you have 60 miles to go". So I climbed to FL130. Actually the TB20 can do better than 300fpm at 11,000 feet but obviously the speed drops off and it's always good to look after engine management (cooling) if there is no hurry.

Almost the entire flight was VMC on top, mostly above a thin broken layer. **This is what IFR flight is all about: mission capability limited only by aircraft performance, and low enroute workload.** It's not for everybody, and I much prefer VFR for the view when the weather is OK. However, about 50nm before Prague I encountered gradually rising tops, entered IMC and eventually started to collect some rime ice, perhaps 1mm every few minutes. The stormscope was showing some returns too, to the right of my track.

I had been watching this from much further back when still in VMC; looking out for the back of that cold front which I was catching up with (the WX500 displays returns up to a 200nm radius) and could see some large towering cumulus in the distance. I was not going to fly into those, but both the stormscope returns and the towering cumulus appeared to be to the right of my track. I find the stormscope good for direction - usually spot on when flying in VMC with groups of CBs in the distance - and less accurate for the distance which can be out by a factor of two. If I had not seen the clouds a few minutes before I would have asked for a 20 degrees left "due to weather" just in case.

The rime ice was pretty harmless and I have a TKS de-iced propeller which I use in any freezing IMC (switch it on a minute before entry) but it's always best to make decisions soon rather than late so I asked for a descent to FL090 "due to icing". Prague radar gave me a descent to FL100 which I initially accepted and which turned out to be fine since the cloud base was about FL105 and it got me out of the cloud. At about 30nm to run I received a descent to FL080, then FL060, then 4,000 feet, then (given good VMC) I was offered a visual approach or ILS and being lazy I chose the ILS.

The Prague ATIS gave the LOMKI 1S STAR which was the correct one for RWY 24 and for my route. Prague has a huge array of STARs and SIDs, and three or four ILS runways, so I had asked one of the preceding (German) sectors to phone Prague and get me the current runway so I could get the paperwork in order.

There was a very useful 40-50kt of tailwind for most of the flight and on the descent to 4,000 feet I recorded the highest ground speed I ever saw on the TB20, 211kt, corresponding to about 165kt IAS.

ATC was obviously happy with this but as my speed dropped off quickly upon levelling off, they asked me to keep my speed up because of other traffic. So I intercepted the localiser at the gear limiting speed (130kt) and slowed down on the glideslope. The unchallenging landing (the runway wasn't exactly short) was followed by a very long taxi (behind a FOLLOW ME vehicle) to the "old terminal" which is reserved for private aircraft, mostly small jets. The entire flight, including the ILS, was flown on autopilot. Airborne time was 3:35.

I asked for avgas while still taxiing; this trick helps at a lot of places but here the Ground controller was not able to help. However, the airport handling bus turned up within minutes and I told him I needed fuel so he organised it; all done very quickly. Tax free avgas is available to "commercial" customers but only on production of an AOC; this appears very common around Europe.

Everything is very easy at the Prague airport. A police officer looks at the passport and you go straight out to a taxi; eight miles and 350 crowns (about £8) takes you to the city centre.

Prague

Prague is a great old Central European city. I will not write what you can find in a travel brochure but thoroughly recommend the city for a visit.

The return flight LKPR-EGKA

Getting out through the GA terminal at Prague airport is easy; you just pay the fees, walk through a security check and get onto the bus.

The filed route was the one provided by CFMU, namely: RAK L984 DONAD T170 RAPET Z23 SULUS L604 FUL Z52 ARPEG Z850 HMM B5 FLEVO R105 PAM L980 REFSO Y76 DET

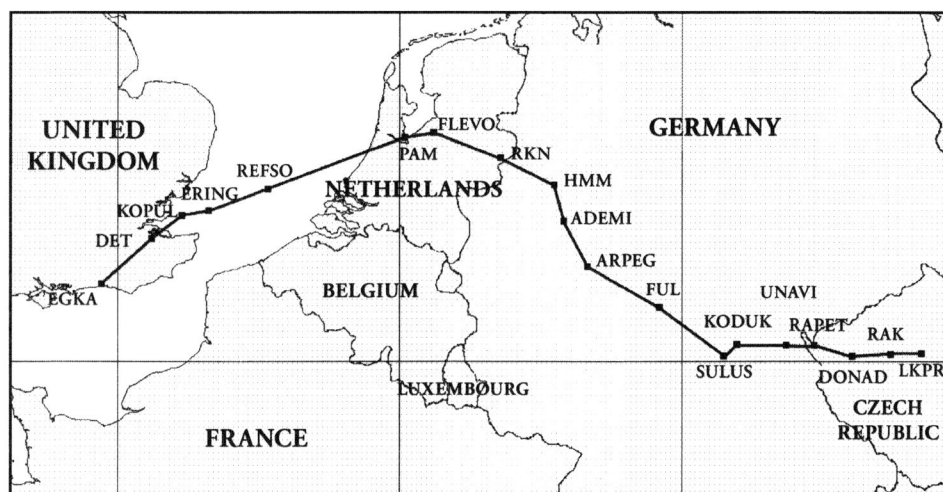

Prague has a dedicated Delivery frequency where you collect your departure clearance while still on the ground. Then start the engine and call up Ground who give taxi instructions to the runway threshold where you do power checks and then they change you over to Tower. The SIDs request an automatic change to radar immediately when airborne but in this case they told me to remain on the Tower frequency.

Current runway (on ATIS) was still 24 and this was used by the heavy traffic, but they offered me 31 since the wind was 310. The holding point for 31 was also usefully very close to the GA parking area. However the offer of runway 31 caught me by surprise since I had not studied the SIDs for 31, so I said I prefer 24 unless I get a radar departure. In reality, arrivals – and to a lesser extent departures – at large European airports tend to be radar vectored but one still needs to be able to fly the SID or STAR if required, at short notice.

The IFR clearance was "Cleared to EGKA, radar departure, squawk 1433, climb 5,000 feet on runway heading". Shortly after departure I was asked to contact radar who gave me a climb to FL100, DCT RAPET, and that was it. Many vectors and DCTs all the way home, at FL100, in pleasant sunshine, VMC on top.

I did ask for a DCT from ARPEG to REFSO, to cut out the large detour in the filed route, but they refused. The route actually flown was reasonably close to that filed, with some short cuts. This time I had 15-25kt of headwind and it took 4:40 airborne time. The TB20 could have made it to Prague and back without refuelling.... just!

London Control was busy and at one stage gave me a "provisional" DCT LAM routing which was soon changed to REFSO TANET DET SFD, later changed to DCT LYD, shortly after which I got a descent to FL060, then (approaching SFD, and still at FL080) was asked to drop out of CAS and contact Shoreham. They passed me some traffic info, comprising of the usual non-transponding contact somewhere below. Curiously they "got rid of me" while I was still in Class A airspace, but this is not unusual.

Arrival at Shoreham was via a standard left base onto runway 20, VFR. I could have flown the NDB/DME procedure but there was no need for this.

The entire trip there and back was straightforward with low workload. It could have been flown under VFR perfectly well on the day (cloud bases around 8,000 feet) but there is much controlled airspace around for which one would really hope to get a transit. There are also terrain issues which would make VFR tricky for much of the year. The cost of the low stress of IFR flight is that one is likely to have less view of the ground.

3 Clockwise through the Greek islands

By Stephen Niechcial

The miserable endless grey of summer of 2007 in the UK made an early autumn trip to the south particularly appealing. The idea had initially come from a proposed *PPL/IR Europe* group trip but then one by one, like the proverbial Little Indians, the participants fell out until it was only ourselves left. The combination of new destinations to savour and new aviation challenges is what flying is all about as far as we are concerned, and this one held the promise of new challenges on almost every front. Flying to the south would involve top of altitude flying capability with mountain conditions. The general scarcity of avgas in the Greek Islands would demand accurate planning with several legs near maximum endurance. Our Grumman Tiger would be loaded to the hilt for those long hot engine-management climbs to 10,000ft plus, and there were the complexities of Greek airspace to fathom with the difficulty of the usual VFR maps not being available. For some people the pleasure of flying means following their fancy and their route as the mood takes them. For me the buzz is in using all my skill and organisational ability to get round the obstacles and complete a demanding itinerary to a smooth schedule. I am really a frustrated airline pilot and went though all the hassle and expense of adding a UK IR to my PPL to prove it! On this occasion my sister in law Kate was coming along with Judith and myself which only added to my determination to deliver the promised tourist sites as efficiently and comfortably as possible.

Preplanning

The essence of achieving this was pre-planning. Evenings for two weeks before departure where taken up with maps, the wonderful Navbox planning programme, and testing out different IFR flight plans on the Brussels computer. Print-outs of most of the airport plates required generated a vast amount of paper to cover thirteen plus destinations and alternates. The aim was to IFR-it clockwise around Europe via Germany, and the Czech Republic as far as the Aegean Islands, VFR-it around the islands themselves and then back to IFR via Croatia, Corsica and France (see map below). Summer as much as winter is a time to capitalise on the advantages of IFR flying as far as I am concerned. The high altitudes give free air conditioning and smooth flying out of surface thermals. The radio contact is more reliable and as you are automatically handed over en-route, you are freed from the need to negotiate yourself across ATZs and other controlled airspace. Once in the air, the 'direct tos' given by ATC often result in shorter distances than VFR. It is also comforting to know for those long sea crossings that you are being watched on somebody's radar nearly all the time.

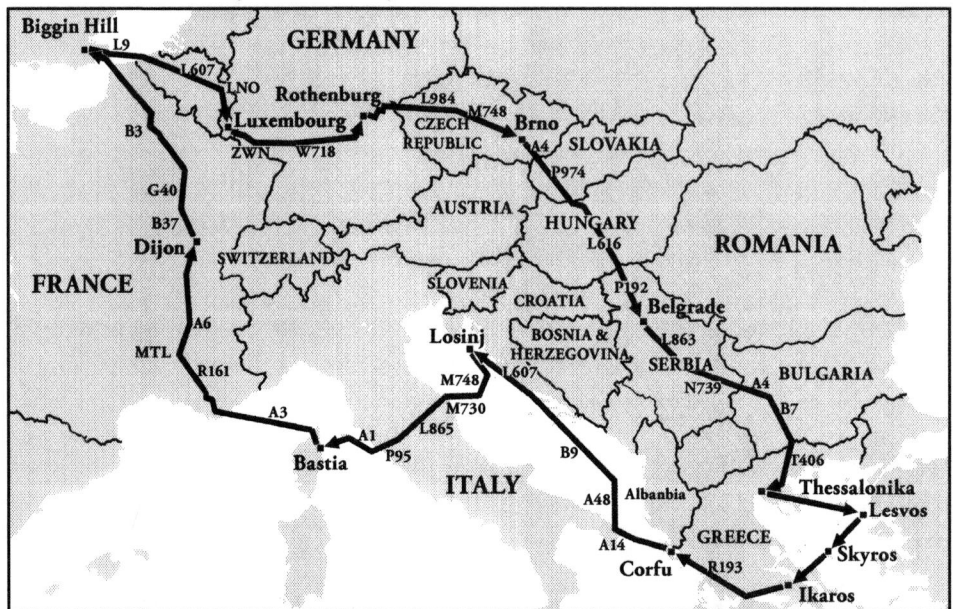

Departure from Biggin Hill

The September Friday of departure dawned a lovely VMC day. On board, we had 13 individual plastic document sleeves, one for each leg containing flight plan, plog, and details of instrument arrival and departure procedures for each of our airports and alternates, together with other essentials such as several litres of oil (often strangely difficult to find abroad), a handheld radio for emergencies and a shiny new yellow Personal Locator Beacon. Taking off from Biggin Hill on one of the brighter days this summer, we were cleared into controlled airspace immediately and began our climb up to FL080, initially on radar vectors and en-route to a lunch and fuel stop at Luxembourg. We were loaded to max and it showed, with our rate of climb falling to less than 300 feet a minute once we had got to 6,000 feet. A gentle ticking off from London Control followed for not pre-warning them that we could not maintain the required minimum climb rate of 500 FPM all the way up. Taxiing to the main apron on arrival we mixed with the many unmarked plain white windowless 747s which seem to be the main traffic here. Presumably they are moving cargo around. Bit scary to think there might be an aviation equivalent to White Van Man!

Rothenburg

Allowing an hour and a half for lunch, fuel and formalities provided a pleasant and not too expensive stop off, and we were off again IFR for our first overnight at Rothenburg, with Nuremberg as the IMC alternate. Rothenburg is served by a very pleasant and friendly club aerodrome with A/G radio (in German only). Cancelling our IFR with about 10 miles to run we joined downwind for 21, and within minutes were in a taxi for the 15 minute ride to the town. Rothenburg is a chocolate-box pretty mediaeval town and tourist trap with traffic free cobbled streets and half timbered, be-flowered façades. We passed a pleasant late afternoon and evening enjoying the views from the long and intact city walls in glorious sunshine from a cloudless sky.

Off next day we faced the normal challenges of how to get into the airways from a VFR-only airstrip. In these circumstances, I always file IFR flight plans back to Heathrow FPU. They are extremely friendly and efficient, phoning back with confirmation or any difficulties. A friendly local pilot had given us one frequency from his chart for controlled airspace entry, while our chart gave another! I spiral climbed attempting to make contact on both dealing with an irritated but barely audible controller telling us she had given us the correct frequency three times already! Once in the airway we established what was to become our crew routine. Judith in the P2 seat dialling frequencies and waypoints into the Garmin 430, Kate in the back following a VFR map, pointing out the ground features and dishing out the in-flight picnic, myself, autopilot engaged, arms folded enjoying the scenery. 'CRM' training eat your heart out!

Czech Republic

Next stop was Brno where we arrived at 15:20 local after a two and a half hour flight. As we all know, when you go into an international airport for the first time, enquiries in advance will only tell you so much, and you do enter into the unknown in terms of unanticipated expense, very variable 'handling', bureaucracy and delays. This one however was hassle free and welcoming but, with total expenses for an overnight stay of about £105, towards the top of the range. Brno itself proved a lively city with a thriving arts scene, jazz festival in the main square, a fine cathedral and a huge, threatening castle in the dungeons of which the Nazi's had persecuted Czech partisans in WW2.

I had located Belgrade as practically the only possible IFR fuelling stop en-route to Greece. A grim airport of surly Serbs, bunkers and a fair walk to a café providing limp sandwiches, but with some of the cheaper fuel on the trip. Back on the tarmac, standing around for family photos resulted in a car full of sinister looking sunglass wearing security guards parking up nearby and fixing us with an unsmiling gaze. Just to make the point, I conducted all pre-flight checks in a particularly leisurely and thorough manner!

Our 'Plan A' for this trip assumed we would get the customary seasonal weather for this area - a stable large high pressure system over middle Europe which would give us the necessary clockwise wind system and light tail winds to manage the long legs we had planned. So far it was coming out fine and we had hardly seen a cloud in the sky. For the next leg, mountains between Sofia and Thessalonica, coupled with a nil wind flight time of almost four hours made it all more critical. The minimum routing level is 10,000 feet which is our max ceiling without oxygen. Even moderate winds could produce mountain waves and downdraughts capable of outstripping the meagre climb performance of a Tiger at that altitude. IR or no IR this would not be a route to tackle in serious IMC. Our luck held good though and we took off with the required conditions. When I filed for FL100, I had not appreciated that the transition altitude for Belgrade was 10,000 ft, which is in fact what we were cleared to fly the whole way. This could have contributed to the IFR/VFR confusion we experienced at our destination as outlined below.

Thessaloniki

Flying over the mountains between Sofia and Skopje it did feel as if we were over territory where very few venture in light aircraft. From our airways corridor of relatively low terrain we saw peaks dramatically rising to out left and right out of the overcast beneath us. It was a long haul, and the approach to Thessaloniki was fraught. The clear blue skies we had enjoyed en-route above the overcast became a thick haze, and, with the evening sun in our eyes, we were in intermittent IMC in mountainous terrain. Meanwhile Thessaloniki Approach apparently had not registered we were on an IFR flight-plan and kept issuing us with visual reporting points not on our IFR chart. Flying to the East of the airport, we were in a region of radar and communication shading by terrain. Altogether not a situation you want to find yourself in at the beginning of a descent into unfamiliar territory. Misunderstandings having been cleared up and communication restored, there then ensued confusion about which of the four runways was in use. We heard a puzzled 737 captain amongst others querying departure and landing runways. Weaving between the hills in the haze and listening, I juggled two or three approach patterns until it was finally clear where we were to circle to land on 28 from a VOR/DME approach to 34. I think all the runway confusion was about attempting to close the main instrument runway for maintenance. Safely down, the next saga was the handler. We had ordered Olympic. Mr. Smart Shades of Swissport insisted it was him, while suggesting he might get us some Jet A1! Hotel Golden Star where we collapsed exhausted was right on the beach at Perea, but was chock-a-block with German tour groups and a trifle Basil Fawlty.

Lesvos

Next morning we set out in more golden sunlight, VFR this time, and using unwieldy military charts (Jeppesen do not stretch this far), for the island of Lesvos near the Turkish coast. In fairness to Swissport their handling on departure was speedy and efficient. Watching tankers below us, we overtook them heading out from the Bospherus. Paradoxically, for VFR in Greece the normal procedure is to either remain in controlled airspace or under fly the airways. This would have stretched our fuel so we were pleased when requests for direct routings were accepted. We approached the island in much higher than forecast winds from the North producing a bumpy watch-you-don't-hit-your-head-on-the-roof ride in the lee of the low mountains. We had a lovely view of the South coast, before rounding a headland and seeing the North-West runway, where I executed an on-the-limits cross-wind landing. A very attractive marshaller in her follow-me van attempted to keep her short skirt under control while hunting around the apron verges in the high wind for the very necessary and substantial concrete tie-downs. The nice Europcar man recommended a sheltered taverna by one of the two huge inland seas, the Gulf of Yera, and our Greek proved just sufficient to order some grilled sardines from said gulf – delicious! We fell in love with Lesvos. Molyvos, the main centre in the North of the island, had a gorgeous view from the Genoese "kastro" over the sparkling bay. A peaceful half hour was also passed in the flower filled courtyard of an ancient convent where elderly nuns tended the beautiful Orthodox chapel and insects hummed.

Skyros

As part of our extensive advance planning I had faxed Skyros airport, primarily a military facility, for permission to visit, but had had no reply. Further telephoning and renewed bursts of faxing between Lesvos airport and Skyros had not produced an answer by the morning we were due to set off, so I began planning a VFR trip to Skiathos as an alternative. When we arrived back at Mytilini airport we learned permission had just come through thanks to the persistence of the friendly director of operations at Mytilini. Skyros airport consists of the usual gigantic military runways built on what looks like a coastal promontory artificially extended into the sea. The high ground extends almost to the threshold from the landward side resulting in a tight right base join to land. There were several hardened pens containing Tornadoes - but no plane spotting photos in this country! We were so glad we got to Skyros because it is truly gorgeous. It is completely different from Lesvos, with spotlessly gleaming white houses looking much more Cycladic than Aegean. Skyros town is clustered on what must be a volcanic plug topped by another kastro and a monastery. The island is blessedly free of tourists, and has an utterly beautiful West coast which we enjoyed in evening sunshine, followed by a glass of retsina at sunset in the port village of Linaria.

Availability of avgas is a major consideration in the Aegean. Very few of the islands' airports have it - none of those we visited. We had anticipated a return to Thessaloniki to re-fuel, a prospect we definitely did not relish. Looking for ideas, I phoned AOPA's Greek representative, Kyprianos Biris, for advice. It is hard to imagine anyone more helpful and generally well informed than Kyprianos – and he speaks immaculate English. He pointed us to a tiny airfield North of Athens, called "Ikaros" which had the precious fluid. (This nomenclature must be ironic, given the sad fate of the mythical

Icarus, crashing to his death for flying too near the sun.) To this trim, hard surface runway field we flew, over more cloud-shrouded mountains, and were served with avgas by Dimos, who single-handedly and very proudly fulfilled every role, from FIS to pruning the immaculate hedges. Apparently it is a favourite stopping off point for American and Canadian flyers, perhaps on business in Athens? It lies in a fertile valley where cotton and maize grow.

We spent rather longer there than we would have liked, because storms were forecast directly over our next destination, Corfu. There was no internet access at Ikaros, and my perpetual and virtually guaranteed fail safe back-up of laptop connected by mobile phone also let me down on this occasion. Without an accurate overview of the weather I was not willing to depart even with the benefit of a stormscope as any diversion would have again got us into complex fuel logistics. Seeing the weather picture later, we could not possibly have dodged the storms. This turned out to be the one weather delay of the whole trip. When we reached Corfu the next day, we learned that the storms had indeed been severe, and were the first rain the island had experienced for three months. Corfu is well used to weekend invasions of light aircraft, and although we were the only one on the tarmac on this day the handling was efficient and quick. We were fuelled, briefed and off again within an hour.

Corfu to Losinj

The flight from Corfu to Losinj (pronounced Low Sheen) was magical. The Dalmatian and then Kvarner islands were a patchwork of forested land and stone shores in a deep blue sea, glimpsed through patches of cumulus from FL100. Again it felt to be very unknown territory. There must be fantastic sailing there, as well as flying. The weather had to be watched however. We were passing through a moderately active cold front and CBs were forecast for the northerly part of the route as well as converging on Corfu from the West as we prepared to depart. Isolated patches of lightning activity showed on the stormscope from time to time - but not close enough to be of concern. The routing was due to take us zig zag via the Italian coast and the BRD NDB, however we were given an almost straight line to Split. In the last 10 miles we passed through what looked like an innocent enough cumulus and got our teeth thoroughly shaken for about 30 seconds. The engine note dropped almost as soon as we entered cloud, which I attributed to the turbulence. However on exiting to clear air, the note remained low (but steady) and we were 20 knots down on airspeed. Looking round the cockpit revealed the fuel primer had been shaken slightly open from the locked position. A new one on me! Descending over the myriad islands, the NDB approach brings you to the middle of the runway and at right angles to it. You then turn one way or the other for a downwind to land at an airport of contrasts. A wooden shack 'departure lounge' that probably went back to the thirties is side by side with a state of the art ATC and flight briefing facility, surly fuellers but a friendly immigration officer. I could not really work the place out as at 900 metres nothing very large could get in and there did not appear to be any scheduled flights. On the other hand, there was very little sign of other GA activity either. The cheapest avgas of the trip was had here at about £0.83 a litre but JET A1 was NOTAMed as off for a considerable period. Within 30 minutes of touch down we were in a taxi.

Losinj is an object lesson in how to absorb tourism while maintaining the natural beauty people come to see. The main town, Mali Losinj, has a population of no more that 7,000, yet the island supports 32,000 beds for the mainly German and Italian tourists. The emphasis is on water sports, walking the excellent network of paths, and boating. We took a trip to the picturesque neighbouring island of Ilovik where eager fish leapt up to devour the remains of our picnic thrown from the boat.

After three days we reluctantly tore ourselves away and flew across Italy to Bastia on Corsica. Unable to accept FL120 meant a slightly longer route via ANC, BOL and Gilio but the air was calm and the visibility almost unlimited. The Elba corner was cut off and we became number one for the VOR/DME approach mixing it with the usual weekend influx of 737s and Airbuses. We explored the citadel and the old harbour, and were grateful to return to French cuisine as well as driving up to mountainous Corte.

Our next and final stopping off point was lovely Dijon. Back now to more familiar weather as low cloud came down to meet us. Time to watch the stormscope again as we were outrunning a storm which eventually held us prisoner to torrential rain in the middle of Dijon about an hour after we landed.

Return to Biggin Hill

Dijon to Biggin Hill was the last leg. The one ATC delay of the trip put back our planned departure 45 minutes - no doubt because we were flying the Paris TMA at rush hour. We departed in 800 metres of fog (remembered that nasty arrester cable just in time!), and flew through layered clouds near the freezing level requesting a couple of track diversions for CB avoidance. The French landscape beneath was magical with all the dips and valleys in-filled by fog as if by the hand of a celestial poly-filla. Our arrival was both dramatic and ignominious. The fog which had lain picturesquely in the valleys of Burgundy had thickly blanketed Biggin all morning, and was only at minimums by the time I flew down the ILS, scanning the murk for the lights of runway 21. Once smoothly on the ground, braking did not feel right and as we lost rudder authority we began to execute a series of graceful slow speed circles on the runway. A bizjet was coming down the ILS, and ATC began asking us with increasing urgency whether we needed assistance. We did. We had a braking problem and, as steering on an AA5 is by differential braking, we also had a steering problem. I just managed to manoeuvre the plane at a strange angle and walking pace onto a taxiway whence it uncontrollably rolled onto the grass. Assistance arrived in the shape of a group of firemen, who pushed the plane into a convenient corner, brake fluid leaking from the starboard brake calliper. The brake pad had apparently broken up, allowing the piston to travel beyond its intended limits. Fortunately, no other damage was incurred. We uttered thanks to a guardian angel watching over us. It would have been an altogether different story if this had happened on some small Greek runway with no engineering facility. We tend not to be superstitious, but this was after all our 13th landing! We had flown 32 tacho hours and had an experience which could only be done by light aircraft. The only sadness was that we did not have the company of other *PPL/IR Europe* pilots, but then there is always next year…

Epilogue

PPL/IR *Europe* in Europe

By Paul Draper

PPL/IR *Europe* has, since 1993, provided private pilots with a way of exchanging knowledge and experience about instrument flying. In contrast to professional pilots, who are supported by the organisation they work for, private pilots are left to their own devices, and **PPL/IR Europe** seeks to remedy that situation. We have members in Belgium, Cyprus, Denmark, France, Germany, Greece, Ireland, Iceland, Italy, Netherlands, Norway, Portugal, Singapore, South Africa, Spain, Sweden, Switzerland and USA, and a growing number in all these countries fly on FAA licences.

Our activities in mainland Europe, aside from enlarging the membership among pilots who are based there have, particularly since 2002, become increasingly involved in matters with the regulatory authorities where we are recognised as a specific European-wide body with a contribution to make to the ever increasing amount of regulation forthcoming. This arises from the considerable expansion of commercial air transport (CAT) with low cost airlines expanding at a prodigious rate and spreading to many of the airports we use. We need to be able to safely intermix with this CAT and to ensure we do not encounter the major problems apparent in the UK where most regional airports are not now easily and economically accessible to our type of activity. In addition whilst in our early years we had much to do with the UK's Civil Aviation Authority (CAA), it is the case that most of their activity is now acting as an agent for the European Aviation Safety Agency (EASA). We also engage with the UK's Department for Transport (DfT) Aviation section, which is increasingly involved with the European Commission (EC) and EASA.

It is essential we interface with the regulators in this age of increasing control of our activities. This means we engage with various of them including the EC, EASA, Eurocontrol, European Civil Aviation Conference (ECAC) and the Single European Sky Air Traffic Research project (SESAR).

There are considerable differences in regulation between the various regulating authorities in the EC Member States and as EASA gradually takes over the role of regulator for all States, it is important to attempt to ensure commonality of treatment throughout all States; not an easy task and it will take much time and effort to achieve on a basis that we regard as acceptable to our members. Our involvement in such matters is crucial to our interests as a relatively small group of private pilots who mix with commercial operators under IFR.

As an organisation, we are corporate members of Europe Air Sports (EAS) and of the Aircraft Owners and Pilots Association (AOPA); most of our members are also personally members of AOPA. These two bodies are the officially accredited representatives of GA with the European Aviation Safety Agency (EASA), and we work with both, and sometimes directly with regulators, to lobby on the specialised topics that concern European GA IFR pilots. We are also corporate members of the Royal Aero Club (RAeC) and the General Aviation Safety Council (GASCo).

The focus of *PPL/IR Europe* is firmly on the needs of the private pilot who exercises his or her privileges under IFR. These needs are as different from those of commercial operators as they are from the needs of the private VFR pilot, and *PPL/IR Europe* is the only organisation that specifically addresses these needs.

The future of instrument flying

By Jim Thorpe

Attempting to predict the future of anything exposes the author to infinitely more prospect of embarrassment than acclaim. Nonetheless prospective instrument pilots inevitably want to assess whether the rating will open up future opportunities which are proportionate to the effort and cost involved. Here then, are my hostages to fortune which might at least help the reader to form judgments of their own.

The world has taken on board the so called green issues. Having taken little interest at all for many decades the chattering classes now pay lip service to the need to address green issues without truly accepting that it will impact on their own lifestyle to a significant degree. It is hard to know how this will play when people have to accept real changes in their core lifestyle rather than taking actions which only have a very peripheral impact. It has to be said that flying a powered light aircraft is unlikely to ever be a truly green activity. On the other hand the impact is minimal compared with that of 'non essential' road transport. One might therefore consider that the degree to which GA will be affected will be similar in magnitude to the changes in a whole raft of non-essential activities which consume resources. If we take a reasonably short time scale say 10 years it seems unlikely that flying will be seriously curtailed by direct environmental measures although these may impact upon costs so as to reduce the appeal of recreational flying.

Are there factors which impinge more on instrument flying than on GA in general? The answer has to be yes on a number of fronts. We need airfields with approach aids whereas much of GA could operate with very limited facilities. The proliferation of low cost commercial carriers is a disincentive to flying since the cost disparity between them and using a light aircraft is so great. These carriers use secondary airports and they continue to squeeze out GA, sometimes directly but more often with landing and parking pricing, time consuming administration and difficulty in getting slots. On the positive side the availability of GPS approaches will open up many new airfields. Although Europe has been very slow compared with the USA it does seem likely that there will in time be a net gain in the number of useful airfields with instrument approaches.

Security precautions have become very onerous and arguably of minimal benefit at major airfields and this ethos have trickled down with silly and variable restrictions at smaller airfields. At the moment this is at the level of irritation rather than serious disincentive. It may even be that in time the disproportion between real security and the convenience to the law abiding traveller will be recognised. On balance I incline to regard this as a minor issue.

There has always been a certain resistance among airlines and commercial pilots to having private pilots share the same airspace. To date this has not developed into a serious threat and the fact that the private IR is identical to the commercial IR remains a good defence. Ironically if attempts to have some lesser qualification with privileges to enter airspace used by commercial traffic succeed this may make this threat more real. My opinion is that as long as there is no high profile accident we will continue to enjoy the current privileges but this is a threat that could develop very quickly indeed should some unfortunate incident or incidents occur.

For several decades there has been minimal development of aircraft capabilities and the average age of the GA fleet has increased with the majority dating back 30 or more years. We now have significant sales of new aircraft with rather greater capabilities than those they replace. This is a positive development and as these aircraft depreciate and are offered on the second hand market access to more capable aircraft will become more affordable. On the other hand the viability of the very cheap old aircraft is now in doubt. The requirement, be it practical or regulatory for panel mount approved GPS, Mode S transponders and other equipment mean that it makes no economic sense to re equip aircraft where the avionics refit might cost more than the value of the airframe. My guess is that the days of something like a 1980 Cessna 172 as a viable IFR machine are numbered. The cost of entry is going to rise and availability of truly IFR capable machines, never very good in the rental or group ownership sectors will get worse. On the other hand the appeal and operational capability of those aircraft that do exist will be significantly greater. It might be viewed as the cost / reward balance remaining similar but the price of entry rising significantly.

Initial and recurrent training is not in good shape at the moment. Few schools make any real concession to catering for the PPL as opposed to CPL IR. It is getting ever more expensive to train in the UK and facilities such as practice approaches are harder to find as regional airports accept more commercial traffic. On the other hand simulators are becoming more realistic, cheaper and can be used for a considerable portion of the course. As Europe-wide pilot licensing becomes a reality it may be that most training will move to parts of Europe where costs and resources are more readily available. It would appear that the theory syllabus, long a bone of contention, will be much simplified. There are some interesting new aircraft, diesel or Rotax powered coming along which could significantly reduce training costs. Overall it would seem that training is an area where we could hope for improvements but it is too early to discern a clear trend. Attracting significantly more people to the instrument rating is a sure way to improve facilities of all kinds. Businesses will after all respond to market opportunities.

Concern as to the future of N-registered aircraft based in Europe and hence the usefulness of the FAA instrument rating rears its head from time to time. I have personally heard senior European officials say that this practice is unacceptable. Whether this will translate into the political will to deal with the likely backlash from those affected is another matter. My view for what it is worth is that the antipathy within Europe to things American is sufficiently strong to make a ban or restrictions likely. However, assuming a degree of rationality both sides could achieve their objective. It costs a significant amount to keep up a US trust in order to own an N-registered aircraft and this provides no direct benefit. Providing there was a reasonably easy way for US registered aircraft to migrate to a European register with acceptance of their existing modification state then owners could accept the change. The same would apply if there was an acceptable way for holders of FAA instrument ratings to obtain a European rating. My guess, and it is a guess, is that N-registered aircraft will be banned but that acceptable means of migration will be provided. Thus although hardly welcome this will prove to be less of an issue then has been predicted.

It seems likely that the great majority of prospective pilots undertake training with the idea that they will go places. Taking the wife or girlfriend for lunch at Le Touquet keeps the prospective PPL motivated through the vagaries of the training process with its bad weather hold ups, battered aircraft, variable standards of instruction and the inevitable expense. On the other hand there are huge satisfactions in the achievements along the way. The newly qualified PPL soon discovers that the practical transport potential of their qualification is limited by weather, the complexity of the process and by availability of suitable aircraft. It is unsurprising that the great majority of pilots give up soon after qualifying. The more determined pilots address the issues by gradually building experience or qualifications. Perhaps they purchase a share in an aircraft. However the end point for anyone who wants seriously to use a light aircraft for transport will be the realisation that they need an instrument rating and an aircraft with considerably more capabilities than the machines they are used to. If they can envisage surmounting these hurdles they will find that the complexities of the IFR system and the need to stay current may still make the effort / reward balance too heavily weighted towards effort.

Does this mean terminal decline for IFR flying. I take a positive view. The potential upside is the large number of people who want to fly and go places. Significant numbers of people have adequate disposable income but they have expectations which flying must be able to deliver. Aircraft are now available with autopilots and GPS capability which makes flying easier. These aircraft look more like a quality car and are more likely to be acceptable to family and friends who are motivated by travel rather than flying. There is a good chance that a more achievable European instrument rating will emerge which does not compromise on the skill levels needed to operate safely and enjoyably but does eliminate the less than useful historical baggage. There is a good chance that GPS based instrument landing systems will open up a whole range of airfields which could not justify the cost of traditional terrestrial approach aids. IFR flying is hardly likely to ever be cheap but there is the potential for the benefits to match the cost and for significantly more pilots to gain the qualification. If this virtuous circle can gain momentum then business will start to deliver training, handling faculties, aircraft shares and other resources which in turn make the activity more practical and enjoyable.

PPL I/R Europe has been working towards this objective for many years. To badly misquote Winston Churchill 'This is not the end, it is not even the beginning of the end but it may just be the end of the beginning'. We have reached the stage where our voice is being heard and there are early signs of improvements in facilities and procedures. With sustained effort over several years there is a good chance that many more people will find the instrument rating attractive and the facilities needed for an instrument rated pilot firstly to train and then to fly both usefully and enjoyably will improve and expand.

Index

Index